The Big Cat Diary

The Big Cat Diary

A Year in the Masai Mara

Brian Jackman & Jonathan Scott

with additional research and photography by Angela Scott

BBC BOOKS

For Annabelle and Angela with love and gratitude

Acknowledgements

We wish to thank the governments of Kenya and Tanzania, the Narok County Council who administer the Masai Mara, and the Maasai people for their generous support during this project. Our Commissioning Editor, Sheila Ableman, Art Director, Frank Phillips, Copy Editor, Romilly Hambling, Project Editor, Anna Ottewill and DW Design, London all played a major role in ensuring the success of *The Big Cat Diary*.

The following books proved particularly useful, although the authors remain blameless for any inaccuracies in the text, or for the inevitable simplifications made in interpreting their work:

Caro, T.M, *Cheetahs of the Serengeti Plains: Group Living in an Asocial Species,*
The University of Chicago Press, 1994

Polking, F., *Leoparden: Die geheimnisvollen Katzen Steinfurt* Tecklenborg Verlag, 1995

Scott, J.P., *The Leopards Tale* Elm Tree Books, 1985

Scott, J.P, *The Great Migration* Elm Tree Books, 1988

Scott, J.P., *Painted Wolves* Hamish Hamilton, 1991

Scott, J.P., *Kingdom of Lions* Kyle Cathie, 1992

This book is published to accompany the BBC television series
The Big Cat Diary, broadcast in 1996.
Series Producers: Robin Hellier and Keith Scholey
Published by BBC Books, an imprint of BBC Worldwide Publishing,
BBC Worldwide Limited, 80 Wood Lane, London W12 0TT

First published 1996
© photographs and concept Jonathan Scott
© text Brian Jackman
The moral rights of the authors have been asserted
ISBN: 0 563 38752 1
All photographs by Jonathan and Angela Scott
Maps by Michael Hill
Set in Bembo and GillSans
Printed by Cambus Litho Limited, East Kilbride
Jacket printed by Lawrence Allen Limited, Weston-super-Mare
Colour reproduction by Colour Origination Limited, Weston-super-Mare
Bound by Hunter and Foulis Limited, Edinburgh

Photograph on page 1: A four-month-old lion cub from the Ol Kiombo pride.
Photograph on page 2: A Serena male cheetah.

Contents

Author's Note

Few people know the Masai Mara National Reserve more intimately than Jonathan Scott, who has spent the greater part of his working life photographing and writing about its magnificent predators. Twenty years ago, when we were both new to the Mara, we worked together on a book called *The Marsh Lions*, a true-life account of the lions of Musiara Marsh. So, when the BBC suggested that I write a book to accompany its *Big Cat Diary* television series I leapt at the chance to team up again with Jonathan and return to the land where the marsh lions roamed.

To present a complete and up to date portrait of the Mara we decided on a diary format which would describe a full year in the life of the reserve and its big cats, leading up to September 1996 so that the climax of the story would coincide with the spectacular migration of wildebeest and zebra through the area and the filming of the series.

Like the television series, we particularly wanted to focus on the day-to-day lives of individual lion prides and leopard and cheetah families rather than describe big cats in general terms. However, this presented several problems. For a start, the text for the book had to be ready by March 1996 – five months before filming had begun! This meant that we could not be certain which cats the camera crews would follow, although we had a good idea. We knew that the Bila Shaka lion pride were strong contenders, as were the two leopards Beauty and Half-Tail and a number of cheetahs that Jonathan had been observing in the Mara Triangle.

In the end, it was decided to make the first six months of the book as factual as possible, relying on first-hand observations made by Jonathan and Angela Scott during their regular visits to the reserve between October 1995 and March 1996. Where this was not possible, as in the latter part of the story from April to October 1996, we had to fall back on informed conjecture.

In doing so, we have relied on two decades of personal observation in the bush to fill the gaps in a way that is both credible and scientifically authentic, and we have gone to great lengths to portray the Mara and the lives of its big cats as honestly as possible. Our efforts will have been worthwhile if the resulting account conveys even a little of the majesty of Kenya's greatest wildlife stronghold.

Brian Jackman

Above: The four Bila Shaka lionesses returning to the croton thickets along the Bila Shaka lugga with their three-month-old cubs one morning after feeding on a kill. Lionesses in a pride are related and often come into season at the same time. This is particularly apparent when new males take over a pride territory and kill the cubs sired by the previous coalition. The females then come into season and breed with the new males. When there is a big age discrepancy among cubs, the smaller cubs are at a disadvantage at kills.

Introduction

The Masai Mara National Reserve is by far the best known and most beautiful of Kenya's many wildlife strongholds. It is one of the last places in Africa where huge concentrations of big game can still be seen: elephant, black rhino, buffalo and, above all, lion. Nowhere else are lions so numerous. In all, 22 separate prides roam the Mara's plains, some with more than 40 members.

Africa's other big cats – the leopard and the cheetah – are also abundant, making the Mara a wildlife film-maker's dream. Throughout the year its high, rolling grasslands present a never-ending pageant of predators and plains game. And as July approaches, when the migrating Serengeti wildebeest pour into this kingdom of lions in their hundreds of thousands, the scene is set for the greatest wildlife spectacle on earth.

The Mara is unique among Kenya's national parks and reserves in allowing 'off-track' driving, giving the freedom to create your own path across the plains and get closer to the big cats than is possible elsewhere. But this privilege is not without its hazards – all it takes is one heavy downpour to turn the Mara's black cotton soils into a slippery nightmare in which it is all too easy for a vehicle to sink up to its axles.

It was the Maasai, the nomadic cattle people of the East African plains, who named the sea of grass between the Isuria escarpment and the Loita Hills. In their language Mara means 'spotted'. So the Mara is the spotted country, the stippled land – like a cheetah's pelt, which is how the plains must once have looked before regular burning of the grass and an increasing elephant population together opened up most of the savannah woodlands.

For two hundred years this was the home of the Maasai, but towards the end of the last century their cattle were annihilated by rinderpest and the tribe itself was stricken by smallpox. Soon the Maasai clans were scattered. Their enkang-iti (stockaded villages) lay empty and the land reverted to the wild.

This was the Mara that the first Europeans saw: an earthly paradise inhabited only by teeming herds of game and a few honey hunters. The next few decades saw the heyday of the professional hunters, the *Out of Africa* era of Denys Finch Hatton and Karen Blixen, when rich westerners would pay handsomely for the chance to bag a black-maned Mara lion.

After the Second World War the Mara lay wide open to exploitation. Shooting became an uncontrolled free-for-all and, with the gradual return of the Maasai, cattle encroached as far as the tsetse fly would allow. But in 1948 the Mara Triangle – 520 square kilometres of land between the Isuria escarpment, the Mara River and the Tanzanian border – was made a national reserve.

Above: Mang'aa (left) and Taratibu at six months of age, resting on rocks along Fig Tree Ridge. Leopard cubs tend to stay together during their early months, sleeping, playing and waiting for their mother to return from hunting. Taratibu was killed by a lioness in 1995. Mang'aa is now independent from his mother, Half-Tail, who has a new litter of cubs, of which one has survived to date.

In 1961 a further 1300 square kilometres was added and the whole area became the Masai Mara National Reserve. It happened just in time. When the killing stopped in that year fewer than ten male lions remained on the Keekorok Plains. In 1984, bowing to pressure from the Maasai for the return of vital water holes and dry-season grazing grounds, the government degazetted 162 square kilometres of the reserve, effectively reducing the size of the Mara by one-tenth.

Since then other changes have overtaken Maasailand. The modern world is closing in. Great wheat ranches now reach out along the road from Narok to the very edges of the Mara. Maasai children go to school, grow up and put aside their red cloaks and long-bladed spears to become doctors, lawyers and MPs. Yet even in the midst of progress the Mara has survived, a vast sweep of old, wild Africa as it used to be – more than 1500 square kilometres of open grassland, seasonal watercourses and riverine forest where plains game and predators wander freely in their old abundance.

Today, the Mara is one of the most popular tourist destinations in Africa, attracting more visitors than the pyramids of Egypt. The money they bring – tourism is Kenya's primary source of foreign exchange – exceeds US$500 million a year and is the best possible guarantee for the reserve's survival. And, despite the proliferation of lodges, tented camps and tourist vehicles, the Mara remains true to itself – a wildlife showcase without equal for the big cats of Africa.

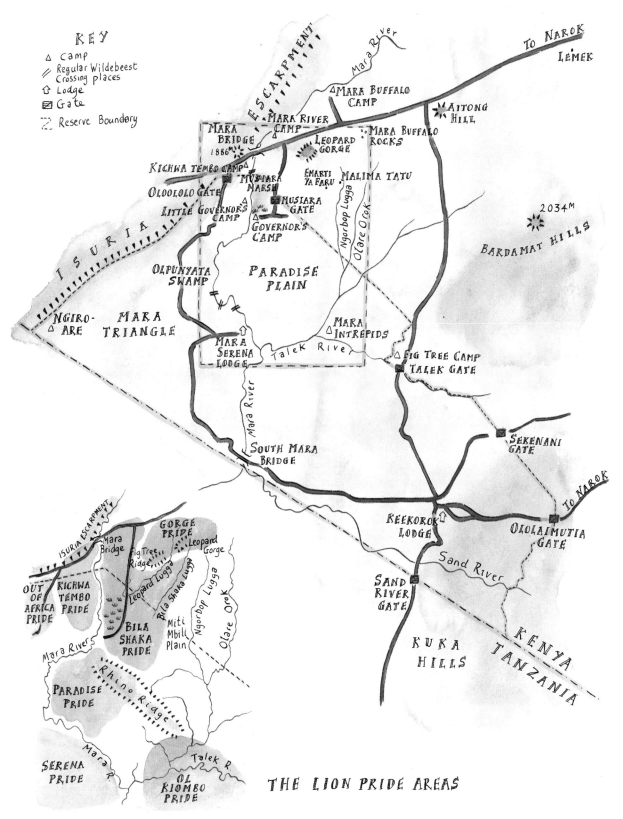

THE MASAI MARA NATIONAL RESERVE

KEY
△ Camp
∥ Regular Wildebeest Crossing places
⇧ Lodge
⌧ Gate
⌇ Reserve Boundary

To Narok
Lemek

Mara River

△ Mara Buffalo Camp

✳ Aitong Hill

ESCARPMENT

Mara River Camp △

Mara Buffalo Rocks

Mara Bridge 1886ᴹ ✳

Leopard Gorge

Kichwa Tembo Camp △

Emarti Ya Faru

Malima Tatu

Oloololo Gate

Musiara Marsh

Musiara Gate

Little Governor's Camp

2034ᴹ ✳

Governor's Camp

ISURIA

BARDAMAT HILLS

Ngorbop Lugga

Olare Orok

Olpunyata Swamp

PARADISE PLAIN

Ngiro-are △

MARA TRIANGLE

Mara △ Intrepids

Mara Serena Lodge ⇧

Talek River

△ Fig Tree Camp
⌧ Talek Gate

Mara River

Sekenani Gate ⌧

South Mara Bridge

To Narok

Keekorok Lodge ⇧

Ololaimutia Gate ⌧

Sand River

Sand River Gate ⌧

KUKA HILLS

KENYA
TANZANIA

THE LION PRIDE AREAS

ISURIA ESCARPMENT

Mara Bridge

GORGE PRIDE

Leopard Gorge

Fig Tree Ridge

Leopard Lugga

Bila Shaka Lugga

OUT OF AFRICA PRIDE

KICHWA TEMBO PRIDE

Ngorbop Lugga

Olare Orok

Mara River

BILA SHAKA PRIDE

Miti Mbili Plain

Rhino Ridge

PARADISE PRIDE

Mara R.

Talek R.

SERENA PRIDE

OL KIOMBO PRIDE

Land Of The Lion

Chapter 1

October 1

Musiara Marsh

Dawn comes up fast in the Mara. Only an hour ago the world was still wrapped in velvet darkness. Zebras drifted like ghosts across the road to Governor's Camp and the eyes of impala caught in the beam of the headlights swam like shoals of green fishes among the stunted acacias. But already the night sky is being rolled back from behind the Loita Hills to the east as the stars die and the air shivers to the rumble of lions.

Soon afterwards, in a silence broken only by the song of white-browed robin-chats and the distant throbbing of doves, the sun rises like a distended blood-red bubble, quivers briefly and then breaks free of the horizon, catching the horned shape of a topi antelope in silhouette against a wash of crimson light. A new day has begun in the Mara.

The topi stands alert and motionless, staring intently towards the open grassland beyond Musiara Marsh. Its whole body seems to tremble with scarcely-concealed tension – a sure indication of a predator not far off.

Sure enough, out in the open maybe 400 metres from the topi, a lion is walking among the termite mounds. It is not interested in the topi. It walks with the unhurried swagger of a full-grown pride-male safe in the heart of its territory, and from time to time it roars, staring all the while towards the riverine forest that follows the meandering Mara River.

The lion calls again. First, the long-drawn-out groan, repeated perhaps half a dozen times, then the husky, deep-throated grunts, fading, fading…. It is the most thrilling sound in Africa, and every day in the Mara begins with this thunderous greeting.

When a lion roars it does not do so with jaws agape. Rather, it calls with muzzle thrust forward, eyes half-closed in concentration, expelling every last ounce of air from deep down in its chest with such power that the sound can be heard up to eight kilometres away.

Lions begin to roar from the age of about one year onwards, and they roar for a variety of reasons: to keep in contact with other pride members, to advertise territorial rights, or to challenge or warn other lions. Basically, it is the lion's way of saying: 'I am here, where are you?' or 'I am here – beware.'

Previous page: As the dry season draws to an end clouds billow into the sky heralding the onset of the short rains, which usually begin in mid-October and continue through December. The rains signal the time of birth for many species, such as topi, warthogs, gazelles and impala. But there is nothing predictable about the rainy seasons, and sometimes the rains fail completely.

Right: Nomadic male lion, Sand River. All young males are forced from their pride when they are two to three years old. This helps to avoid inbreeding. At four to five years old they are big and powerful enough to make a challenge for a territory of their own. The colour of a male's mane is variable and not all males have fine manes. Males in the Mara and Serengeti sometimes grow dark manes with black chest hair.

Left: Kichwa Tembo pride: lioness and three-month-old cub. A lioness begins to breed when she is three to four years old and may live up to 15-20 years. The normal litter is three or four cubs, which are born in a secluded spot, usually in a patch of forest, dry river bed, marsh or rocky outcrop.

This particular male is one of the Bila Shaka lions, the pride whose territory encircles the rich hunting grounds of Musiara Marsh. The marsh is fed by a spring that seeps out of the high ground just to the north of the reserve. From there it spreads south for nearly two kilometres – a long, green stain of tasselled reedbeds and muddy pools running parallel to the Mara River almost as far as Governor's Camp.

The pride's name, Bila Shaka, means 'without doubt' in Swahili, a reference to the fact that even after the long rains – when the grass is high and the big cats are hard to see – you are sure to find some of them resting among the green and orange croton thickets of Bila Shaka lugga, three kilometres east of Musiara. Alongside the lower reaches of the lugga, or seasonal watercourse, lies a level tract of open ground where topi, impala and buffalo sometimes gather to feed; and it is here, on the overgrown banks of the surrounding watercourses, that the four Bila Shaka lionesses love to hide during the hottest hours of the day.

Although the dry-season territory of these Musiara lions is one of the smallest in the Mara, it is during the dry months that the marsh comes into its own. At this time it becomes a magnet for migrating wildebeest and zebras, drawing them in from the waterless plains. The Bila Shaka lions learned this long ago and lie in wait in the tall reeds. There are days when the pride may pull down three or four animals in a single morning, then stretch out beside the hollowed carcasses to sleep off the effects of their feast, panting in the hot sun while flies crawl over their bloated paunches. Yet no matter how many kills the lions make, the thirsty herds must still come to drink.

Six kilometres to the south, in a beautiful area of open plains and dense riverine thickets beyond the high, grassy contours of Rhino Ridge, live the Paradise lions, one of the largest prides in the northern Mara, led by three fierce and huge-bodied males. These are the buffalo killers who regularly pull down full-grown Cape buffalo bulls – the lion's most dangerous prey – and enjoy a glut of easy kills when the migratory herds cross the Mara River and enter the area known as the Mara Triangle.

Sometimes the Ol Kiombo pride – two adult males and three lionesses with seven large cubs and one small one – also wander as far north as Rhino Ridge, but they spend most of their time south of the Talek River.

North of Musiara Marsh a shy group of lions known as the Gorge pride hide up in the acacia thickets and rocky outcrops of Fig Tree Ridge and Leopard Gorge, just outside the reserve boundary. Theirs is traditionally a small pride, a diffident alliance that has been forced to take its chances amongst the Maasai tribesmen rather than venture into Bila Shaka territory.

To the west, on the opposite bank of the Mara River, the plains country of the Kichwa Tembo pride laps at the foot of the Siria escarpment; and from there, beyond the Sabaringo lugga and heading deeper into the Mara Triangle, you enter the Out of Africa pride's low-lying hunting grounds, which in turn give way to the territory of the Serena pride. And so it continues, a mosaic of lion fiefdoms staked out across the reserve from the escarpment to the Sand River, with sufficient prey to support a density of one adult lion in every five square kilometres.

Territories vary considerably in size. Some prides occupy areas as small as 12 square kilometres, while on the plains around Keekorok Lodge in the southeast powerful coalitions of three or four pride males defend territories of up to 100 square kilometres. But not even the largest pride can defend so big an area day after day. Territories often overlap at their edges and boundaries between the prides are fluid, reflecting the seasonal movements of prey or the outcome of power struggles between new alliances and the established order.

The territory of the Bila Shaka lions is no exception. Throughout the dry season, when wildebeest and zebras from the Serengeti flood their home ground, the pride confines its hunting activities almost exclusively to within a few square kilometres of Musiara Marsh. At this time of the year the marsh becomes the core of the pride's kingdom and is defended fiercely against incursions by neighbours and the unwanted attentions of nomadic lions.

Above: The Bila Shaka pride feeding on a buffalo at the edge of Musiara Marsh. Visitors spend much of their time on safari searching for the big cats. There are more than 500 lions in the Masai Mara, and once the wildebeest migration has departed at the end of the dry season they must hunt resident prey species which live in the reserve year round, such as buffalo, topi and warthog.

Living in a pride has many advantages and renders lions unique as the only cats that consort in groups of adult males and females. Hunting as a group enables lions to overpower animals even as big and powerful as adult bull buffaloes, and a pride is far more successful in defending its kills from the more numerous hyenas, which are always on the lookout for an easy meal. But most important of all is the security that pride membership confers on the females. For lionesses and their cubs the pride is life itself.

The pride structure reveals lions to be animals with a surprisingly complex social order. The basis of any pride is a matriarchal continuity of related females − mothers and daughters, sisters and half-sisters, aunts and cousins − born and reared in the same group. Most lionesses live their life in the area where they were born, acquiring by association with older female relatives the vital knowledge that enables them to survive − where to find water and shelter, the safest places to give birth and the best spots for ambushing prey.

Previous page: The Gorge pride is one of the smaller prides, roaming the rocky outcrops and acacia thickets surrounding Leopard Gorge and Fig Tree Ridge beyond the reserve boundary. There are three adult lionesses in the pride, two adult mates and a number of sub-adults and cubs – ten lions in all.

The adult males, too, are often brothers or litter-mates, but they are almost always unrelated to the pride females. Expelled from their natal pride by the time they are three years old, young males form bachelor coalitions and live the shiftless life of nomads until they are old enough to win a pride of their own. Once established, their tenure as pride-masters is relatively brief – perhaps only two or three years before they, in turn, suffer the ignominy of being ousted by younger challengers.

The history of the Bila Shaka lions provides a dramatic insight into the way males affect the pride's fortunes. In the late 1970s the pride was dominated by a trio of magnificent males known as Brando, Scar and Mkubwa. Together with their five lionesses they were known as the Marsh Lions and were the most famous pride in the Mara. Within a few years the number of lionesses in the pride had grown so large that some of the younger ones broke away and claimed the Musiara area for themselves, leaving their older relatives to occupy the Bila Shaka territory to the east.

In 1981 the Marsh males were forced out of the Musiara marshlands by a formidable alliance of incoming nomads. Soon afterwards Brando disappeared, but Scar and Mkubwa crossed the Mara River and established themselves on the Kichwa Tembo Plain, where they joined forces with another Musiara outcast, a legendary veteran known variously as Old Man or Casanova.

Old Man had been one of the largest and most handsome lions ever seen in the Mara. Even in his last years, his muzzle criss-crossed with battle scars and his left eye gouged out in a fight over territory, he was still a magnificent animal. Briefly he and his two companions took over the Kichwa Tembo pride until they, in turn, were vanquished by three younger males.

Meanwhile, a coalition of seven male lions had moved into the Musiara area. None of the safari drivers at Governor's Camp could remember seeing such a powerful alliance as these aggressive four-year-olds, who they nicknamed 'Amin's dictators' (after Uganda's Idi Amin) because of the ease with which they were able to intimidate their rivals. So powerful were the dictators that in no time they had extended their influence, dominating not only the marsh but all the Bila Shaka territory beyond and mating with the lionesses of both prides.

Eventually, intense competition over food and the favours of the females caused a split in the coalition. Four of the dictators remained around the Musiara Marsh pride and three settled down with the remaining Bila Shaka lionesses to the east. But, like medieval kings whose dynasties enjoy a brief golden age, their days of glory were about to end.

During the early 1990s two of the Marsh males took to killing cattle from the Maasai manyattas (stockaded villages) outside the reserve and paid with their lives, leaving their two companions in control of the pride. These two were brothers – one easily recognizable by the deep scar left by a poacher's snare. When the scarred male's brother died of wounds after an ill-fated attempt to take over the Kichwa Tembo pride, it was clear that one male lion alone could not keep guard over Musiara Marsh for ever.

Soon afterwards the snare-scarred male also vanished and was presumed dead, leaving the Marsh pride leaderless and in disarray. One by one the rest of the pride disappeared during the long rains, leaving the bountiful hunting grounds of the marsh strangely deserted. But nature abhors a vacuum, and it was not long before the Bila Shaka lions, their numbers strengthened by the arrival of two blond-maned nomads from the Serengeti, once more reclaimed the marsh.

So, by a strange twist of fate, the Bila Shaka pride – created by outcasts from the Marsh pride in 1981 – had now returned to claim its inheritance. Although their attachment to the shady thickets of Bila Shaka lugga remained unbroken, they were, in effect, the Marsh Lions again, killing buffaloes in the reedbeds and keeping watch from the same ant hills that the five original lionesses had used as lookout posts 16 years earlier.

October 7

Miti Mbili Plain

More than two months have passed since the first of the Serengeti wildebeest arrived from Tanzania, crossing the Mara River to spread out across their dry-season grazing grounds. The grass, so tall and green when they arrived, has long since been reduced to stubble, chomped and trampled by the wandering herds. Even Musiara Marsh has become a shadow of its former self, its reedbeds flattened, its shrunken pools haunted by yellow-billed storks spearing catfish in the newly exposed shallows. Now, dust devils whirl across the land, driven by dry-season winds that hiss among the hollowed galls of the whistling thorns.

Red-chested cuckoos have been crying 'It-will-rain, it-will-rain' in the riverine forest glades, but the mornings have been bright and cloudless. Increasingly, though, in the still afternoons fleets of flat-bottomed clouds have begun to sail across the sky, trailing islands of shadow over the gasping plains, and evenings bring the mutter of thunder in the distant hills. Any day now the time of the short rains will be here, when sudden showers and late-afternoon storms bring the dry season to an end and coax green flushes of fresh grass from the earth.

East of Bila Shaka the grasslands rise in a long, tawny swell, rolling away in the direction of Aitong Hill and the Loita Plains. For many years two trees stood here, side by side. Their twin canopies, clipped short by generations of browsing giraffes, provided safari camp drivers with a prominent landmark when discussing the whereabouts of lions

or cheetahs. Today the two trees (Miti Mbili in Swahili) are long gone, but the older safari guides still refer to the area as Miti Mbili Plain.

The sudden departure of the migrating wildebeest and zebra from one area to the next can leave the plains looking strangely empty. A week ago the Miti Mbili grasslands were black with animals. Now, wherever you look, there are vast empty spaces and bare horizons.

But the emptiness is an illusion. Look again. Quarter the ground through binoculars. Let your eyes run along the immense horizons and down the flanks of the rolling ridges, and everywhere there is life. Here a family of giraffes swim into focus, half-hidden by the acacias on which they are browsing; there, a troop of olive baboons are foraging for green shoots and scorpions under the watchful gaze of the big, dog-faced adult males. Farther off a sudden movement betrays a family of warthogs running in line astern, their tails raised like radio antennae; and, beyond them, scatterings of zebras and Thomson's gazelles with twitching flanks are nibbling at the close-bitten grasses.

In short, all the resident animals that make the Mara one of Africa's most

Previous page: Giraffe are browsers, feeding on acacia leaves, pods and soft thorns which they grasp with their prehensile upper lip and 45-centimetre tongue. They can go for days without drinking if succulent vegetation is available. Male giraffe are heavier and taller than the females, weighing up to 1275 kilograms and standing 5.5 metres tall. There are three sub-species in Kenya, the Masai giraffe (pictured here), the endangered Rothschild's giraffe and the reticulated giraffe of the northern districts.

Below: Olive baboons live in troops of between 20 and 150 individuals wandering over a home range of 20–30 square kilometres. Large troops are usual in the Mara. Baboons are omnivorous animals spending much of the day searching for food. They will eat grass, herbs, seeds, roots, leaves, fruits and berries, bark and sap, honey-comb, freshwater crabs, spiders, scorpions, winged termites, eggs and nestlings, and lizards. Male baboons sometimes kill young antelope and African hares. Young baboons are carried under their mother's chest where they cling to the long hair. At five weeks old they start to ride jockey-style and are weaned at eight months. Baboons roost in trees or among rocky outcrops during the night to avoid predators.

prolific wildlife strongholds are still present, from rare black rhinos, Cape buffaloes and six-tonne elephant bulls to hyraxes, dwarf mongooses and the diminutive dik-dik – an antelope scarcely bigger than a hare.

Later in the year, after the Serengeti herds have marched south, sizeable numbers of wildebeest will still be found scattered across the reserve. Not so long ago even a single wildebeest would have been a rare sight once the Serengeti herds had left. But these residents, numbering between 20,000 and 30,000, are the remnants of the 90,000-strong population that used to migrate to the Mara from another area – the Loita Plains northeast of the reserve. Today, wheatfields and wire fences have changed these northeastern approaches for ever as some Maasai landowners lease their land to farmers, and many of the Loita wildebeest, denied access to their old calving grounds, now remain permanently in the Mara.

October 15

Mara Triangle

The dry-season winds blow unabated across the plains, carrying the dark shapes of vultures in their endless search for carrion. In this land of predators the skies are never empty, and if the plains and thickets are the domain of the big cats and hyenas, the heavens are the realm of the raptors – vultures, eagles, kites, harriers, buzzards, hawks and falcons.

Rare black eagles drift past the rimrocks of the Isuria escarpment, seeking to surprise hyraxes as they bask on their early morning ledges; and bateleur eagles sail over the plains, rocking and tilting on their long wings – hence the name, meaning acrobat or tightrope walker, given to them by the late eighteenth-century French explorer François Le Vaillant. Bateleurs feed mostly on carrion but are also adept at killing reptiles and small animals such as grass rats and small mongooses. They appear to need thermals much less than other large raptors and spend their days patrolling in long, curving flights over the plains. Like the snake eagles to which they are most closely related, their coral-red legs are heavily scaled and they lay a single white egg which takes about eight weeks to hatch – longer than any other African eagle.

The lower airs, too, are alive with wings. African marsh harriers sweep across the grasslands like giant moths. Black-shouldered kites, delicate birds with crimson eyes and immaculate white and dove-grey plumage, hover as expertly as kestrels, and gabar goshawks dash furiously between the thorn trees, jinking and twisting in pursuit of their prey.

High on its perch in the crown of a Balanites tree stands a martial eagle, its spotted ermine underparts fluttering in the breeze like a medieval banner. Martials are the largest of the plains eagles and are easily capable of killing gazelle fawns, dik-dik and monitor lizards. Not far from where the martial keeps watch is a large acacia tree whose flat canopy

Left: Long-crested eagles are common in the Mara, particularly during the rainy season when the rodent population is breeding and grass rats are plentiful. They have white banding on their tails and distinct white wing patches which are visible only in flight. They have a high-pitched cry uttered on the wing.

supports a tawny eagle's nest. Like the martials, the tawny eagles mate for life and often use the same eyrie year after year. Although they scavenge as successfully as any vulture, they raise their young in the dry season when the long grass has been mown down by millions of nibbling mouths, providing less cover for the rodents and other small mammals on which they also feed.

A month ago the tawnies' nest – an untidy pile of sticks – held two chalky white eggs covered with rusty stains and blotches. Both eggs hatched, but only one fluffy white chick has survived. This was the first to hatch and, as is the way with eagles, it killed its younger sibling and heaved it out of the nest. Now, whenever one of the parents flies in with a rat in its talons the lone fledgling gets the whole meal – and it is growing fast.

Of all the sky hunters of the savannah it is the vultures – Africa's dark angels of death – that dominate the wide horizons of the Mara. On a kill, hissing and threatening with bare necks extended, they are sinister creatures indeed. But flight transforms the ghoulish vulture into a creature of matchless, soaring grace.

There are six species of this supreme scavenger in the Mara, each with its own way of devouring the dead. Head and shoulders above the rest stands the lappet-faced vulture, whose powerful beak can rip open a carcass with ease, rendering the viscera more accessible to other carrion-eaters. Like the white-headed vulture it will occasionally kill live prey, including hares, bat-eared foxes and Thomson's gazelle fawns.

Next in the pecking order come white-backed vultures and Rüppell's griffons, whose long, bare necks enable them to reach deep inside the carcass. Unlike the lappets and white-headed vultures, which are territorial and seen mostly in pairs, the white-backs and griffons arrive in droves, greatly outnumbering all other vultures on a kill. Both species are similar in size, but the white-backed vulture has a black bill as opposed to the griffon's ivory bill. The hooded vulture and the Egyptian vulture, with its distinctive yellow face, are smaller birds with thinner beaks designed for picking up scraps and leftovers once their bigger brethren have eaten their fill.

The combined Mara–Serengeti ecosystem supports a population of 40,000 vultures – an airborne sanitation squad that disposes of more than 12,000 tonnes of carrion each year.

The Rüppell's griffons, with their white Tudor ruffs and cold yellow eyes, lead extraordinary lives. Those seen in the Mara are long-distance scavengers from the Gol Mountains, which lie far to the south in Tanzania at the edge of the Serengeti Plains. Hundreds of pairs roost and breed there, preening and squabbling on inaccessible cliff ledges. But every morning, as soon as the sun's rays wash over the cliffs and breathe new life into the thin highland air, the griffons lift off one by one, spiralling from one thermal to the next until they are high enough to glide on the upper airstreams at speeds of around 50 kilometres per hour – fast enough for them to reach the Mara in two hours, gorge on a lion kill and be back in the Gol Mountains before nightfall after a round trip of 150 kilometres or more.

In the Mara, no matter what misfortunes befall the animals, the vultures are the beneficiaries. During the migration, when wildebeest die in their hundreds as they stampede across the Mara River, the bankside trees are thronged with vultures so gorged they can hardly fly. And later, when the Serengeti wildebeest have departed, some griffons still fly north each day as drought takes its toll of the resident herds.

In 1993 the long rains of April and May failed completely. All over Kenya people and animals suffered. By August, Maasai herdsmen living in the Ngong Hills near Nairobi were driving their cows into the heart of the city in a desperate search for grazing. In the Mara hippo pools dried and cracked under the unrelenting sun, and even the zebras – normally so sleek and fat – began to sicken. Young foals died where they stood, providing more food for the vultures.

This year has been better, but still the land has been crying out for rain – and today its prayers were answered. In late afternoon a storm built up over the Mau escarpment, far to the north, raising billowing thunderheads beneath which lightning flickered along the darkening horizon. One moment herds of zebra were wheeling and cantering across the plains in full sunlight, their stripes dazzling against an indigo wall of cloud. The next, it began to rain, the first spots as big as old English pennies, then increasing in intensity until the skyline was completely obscured and all other sounds were drowned by the joyous drumming of a tropical downpour.

An hour later the rain stopped almost as suddenly as it had begun. The storm passed over, rumbling on down into the Serengeti. The dust was laid, and for the first time for months there rose the clean smell of earth freshly slaked. Larks and crowned plovers rose crying into the clear highland air. Volleys of doves hurtled through the golden light. And two nomadic lions that had been lying in the lee of a termite mound stood up, shook the rain from their bedraggled manes and began walking north towards Kichwa Tembo.

Right: Male lion drinking with two one-year-old cubs. Cats have very few sweat glands and must pant rapidly to lose heat, a process called evaporative cooling. Lions often drink after feeding but in dry areas they can survive without water for long periods, relying on the blood and body fluids of their prey and avoiding heat stress by hunting at night.

The Grass Rains

Chapter 2

November 2

Mara Triangle

The two nomadic lions last seen in the rainstorm on 15 October have moved closer to Kichwa Tembo and have been lying up all day near a half-eaten zebra mare in a thicket within sight of Sabaringo lugga, the steep-sided watercourse that winds past Kichwa Tembo Camp.

They are typical of their kind: young four-year-olds with pale, scruffy manes and an air of devilment about them. They look so alike that they are almost certainly brothers, born into one of the Serengeti prides and then driven out as sub-adults three years later when their presence was deemed to be a threat to the supremacy of the adult pride males. Since then they have stayed together for companionship and mutual security, feeding on whatever carcasses they can pilfer from hyenas and cheetahs in between the kills they make themselves.

When the wildebeest migration moved north again to the Serengeti woodlands in July, crossing the Sand River and spilling out across the Keekorok Plains towards Olempito Hill, perhaps these two brothers followed, lured by the promise of easy kills. At any time there may be as many as 70 nomadic lions wandering around the Mara, although not all of them come from the Serengeti. Many are outcasts from the resident prides, forced to live like fugitives until they are strong enough to claim a pride of their own.

Evidently the brothers did not stay long near Keekorok – probably forced to move on by the males of the powerful Keekorok prides. Over the next few weeks, as the wildebeest and zebras swept in dark tides into every corner of the Mara, the two young outcasts trailed in their wake, hiding by day and hunting by night along the margins of pride territories where there was less chance of running into resident males.

Until this point their story followed a pattern similar to that of the resident pair of Kichwa Tembo pride males, who had come north with the previous year's migration.

Previous page: Storm clouds near Mara Intrepids Camp (in the Ol Kiombo pride territory). The onset of the rains is signalled by dramatic storm clouds and spectacular sunsets. The northern Mara receives 1200 milimetres of rain annually, the highest in the Serengeti-Mara ecosystem. This helps provide ideal conditions for a wide variety of resident herbivores which live in the Mara year round, as well as creating a dry season refuge for the migratory wildebeest and zebra, which move north from the Serengeti in June and July to seek food and water.

Right: Nomadic male lions near Gol Kopjes, Serengeti plains. There are fewer lions on the short grass plains than in the savannah woodlands, where resident prey help to ensure a year-round supply of food for the lions, allowing them to stake out permanent territories. Nomadic lions do not belong to a pride and must hunt for themselves or steal from other predators. The migratory herds of wildebeest and zebra provide a moveable feast for the predators, enabling nomadic lions to follow the herds onto the plains during the wet season.

Except that when the Kichwa Tembo males arrived in September 1994 these brothers had joined forces with three other young outcasts whose distinctive dark manes made them easily recognizable.

Together the five nomads were in a much stronger position than this year's newcomers to withstand the challenge of hostile residents. At first they were nervous, running and hiding at the first distant glimpse of other lions. But when the wildebeest returned to the Serengeti in late October the five nomads did not go with them. Instead, as their confidence grew they began to hang around the Mara Serena hippo pools — a low-lying area of oxbow lakes on the west side of the Mara River. During the migration these pools are a favourite watering-place for wildebeest, and even when the herds have gone resident warthog, topi and buffalo continue to frequent the area.

Eventually the five nomads chose to withdraw rather than risk a showdown with the resident Serena lions, but it was not long before they began to covet the territory of the Kichwa Tembo pride and its three lionesses. Two of these lionesses are the daughters of one of the original Musiara Marsh pride — a veteran of 17 years known as the Old One, who was speared by Maasai herdsmen for stock-raiding. Although they are sisters, the Old One's daughters are from different litters, with a two-year age gap between them. The older sister is about eight years old. The younger one is six years old and is the mother of the third lioness.

Until December 1994 two magnificent black-maned males had been the top lions of Kichwa Tembo. There were times when this pair used to cross the Mara River and prowl around Musiara Marsh. In fact years before, when they were still trying to gain a foothold in the area, they had mated with the Bila Shaka lionesses and sired their cubs – only to abandon them and take over the Kichwa Tembo pride.

For a time it seemed that the Kichwa Tembo pride would prosper under them. They mated with the Old One's daughters and sired four cubs. Within a year, however, their reign was cut short by the arrival of the five young nomads. By now the two resident males were old and battle-scarred and, against such odds, had no option but to flee for their lives.

The four cubs they had sired were not so lucky. The sudden, violent arrival of new male lions is always a traumatic time for the rest of the pride. While the fate of the Kichwa Tembo males was being decided the lionesses had watched from a distance. Then, cowed by the intimidating presence of the victorious strangers, they slunk off into the bushes, calling softly to their cubs to follow.

It was no use. One by one the cubs were hunted down and killed with a quick bite to the neck, back or head. There are few sights in nature as pathetic as a dead lion cub, but in the harsh world of the African bush there is no room for sentiment, and even the killing of young lions by their own kind has a purpose, no matter how senseless it may appear to human eyes.

Infanticide reveals the darker side of lion society. It invariably happens when an incoming coalition of nomadic males takes possession of a new pride. At such times any cubs up to a year old face almost certain death. The reason is simple and has a brutal logic.

It is the story of the selfish gene writ large. A male lion has no interest in raising cubs sired by erstwhile rivals but every interest in continuing his own line. Of course the males, driven simply by the sexual imperative, know nothing of this. And the briefness of their time as pride-masters – perhaps no more than a couple of years – accounts for the ruthless urgency of their actions.

The death of cubs causes lionesses to come into heat and mate with their new consorts, greatly increasing the number of cubs pride males can sire in their lifetime. Even so, after a takeover it is normally at least three months before the lionesses can conceive, allowing time for the new order to establish itself.

So it was with the takeover of the Kichwa Tembo pride. The youngest lioness was the first to give birth. Her two cubs were born in March 1995 and, four months later, her mother also produced two cubs.

Soon afterwards the coalition of the five nomadic males broke up. Three drifted back to the Serena hippo pools, where they drove out the incumbent males and took over the lionesses of the Serena pride. This left just two males to guard the Kichwa Tembo pride, which is how things stand at present.

Now, for the third year in succession, history seems to be repeating itself. The two brothers seen this morning with their zebra kill have begun to behave more brazenly, roaring each night across the Sabaringo lugga as if throwing down a challenge to the two Kichwa Tembo pride males. It looks as though another power struggle for possession of the pride has begun – a confrontation that will be repeated all over the Mara in the weeks to come.

November 10

Sabaringo Lugga

The season of the short rains has transformed the Mara. The Keekorok Plains, burnt black by a devastating grass fire in the dry season, are green again. The buffalo wallows have been replenished and the thirsty herds reprieved. Everywhere the frail white tissue-paper flowers that appeared almost overnight after the first heavy showers now shine among the grasses like falls of snow and the termite mounds are adorned at the base by fireball lilies. It is the time the Maasai call ilkisirat, when topi, Coke's hartebeest, warthogs, impalas and Thomson's gazelles all give birth, taking advantage of the sweet new grasses to fatten their gangling babies.

For the ostriches, too, it is the peak of the breeding season. For weeks the handsome black and white males, bare necks and thighs inflamed by lust to a livid pink, have been strutting around their territories, courting passing females and leading them to nest sites where as many as 30 eggs may pile up on the ground.

By early October the Sabaringo lugga had been reduced to a few stinking pools. Then, after a heavy thunderstorm last week, it almost overflowed. So much rain fell that the Mara River rose several feet, pouring over the concrete bridge on the road leading to the Mara River Camp. Now the lugga is running clear again beneath its lush green cloak of wild olives, majestic old fig trees and African greenhearts.

When the figs are ripe the early mornings are alive with flocks of green pigeons and the braying calls of black-and-white-casqued hornbills as they fly overhead on creaking wings. One Maasai legend says they are the souls of lost warriors, members of a raiding party ambushed in the forest and forever trying to find their way home. Schalow's turacos, large green birds with flashing crimson underwings, add their own distinctive cries from the forest canopy – a far-carrying kaar-kaar-kaar that is one of the most evocative sounds of the Mara's riverine woodlands.

The Sabaringo lugga is always a good place for birds, and bearded woodpeckers, double-toothed barbets, Narina's trogons and long-crested eagles are just some of the species to be found here. Noisy parties of green wood hoopoes with long tails and curved red bills explore the tree trunks, winkling out insects from cracks in the bark, and red-necked spurfowl call from their hiding places in the tangled bankside grasses.

Previous page: Thomson's gazelles running from a cheetah. These animals are migratory though they do not migrate such large distances as the wildebeest and zebras. There are 500,000 gazelles in the Serengeti-Mara and they are the primary prey of both the cheetah and the wild dog, as well as being an important prey species for leopard. Male Thomson's gazelles defend a territory by marking it with black tar-like deposits from their facial (pre-orbital) glands which they deposit onto grass stems.

Above: Masai ostrich. Male ostrich have black plumage with red necks and legs; females have brown plumage. Ostrich breed during the short rains when a single male mates with a number of females, all of which lay their eggs in a communal nest. The male incubates the eggs at night, with his black plumage acting as a camouflage in the dark; the dominant female incubates during the daytime. An ostrich egg is equivalent to 24 chicken eggs. There is heavy mortality on eggs and chicks due to predation.

Many mammals, too, frequent the lugga: shy bushbuck with foxy red coats, olive baboons and vervet monkeys. And safari guides from Kichwa Tembo Camp regularly cover the Sabaringo circuit on their early-morning game drives, knowing it to be a favourite resting-place for the Kichwa Tembo lions.

From somewhere beyond the lugga's steep clay banks comes the dull drumbeat of ground hornbills – ungainly black birds as big as turkeys with scarlet wattles and girlish eyelashes – walking deliberately across the grasslands of Kichwa Tembo Plain like a funeral cortège. Ground hornbills may live for 40 years, and this particular group is a familiar sight at Kichwa Tembo. The head of the family is the adult female; distinguished by a blue patch in the centre of her wattle, she is accompanied by her mate, the dominant male. The rest of the group are their sons and daughters.

Although it is not unusual to see ground hornbills take to the air, beating low over the plain on slow, heavy wings, they spend most of their time walking through the grass in search of frogs, lizards, nestlings and grasshoppers. Anything edible will do. Not even terrapins, encased in armour-plated shells, are safe from their sharp pickaxe bills.

The sombre voices of the hornbills can be heard five kilometres away and, at such a distance, sound strangely like human voices. One Maasai folk tale translates their mutterings as a man saying to a woman: 'I want more cows', to which she replies 'You'll be dead before you get them!'

November 25

Kichwa Tembo Plain

Late-afternoon storms continue to refresh the plains, coaxing clouds of winged termites from their earth castles. Aroused by the drumming raindrops, the termites pour into the sky like an eruption from a geyser, a generation of future kings and queens that will never again see daylight after this one brief flight of freedom. On drifting back to earth they discard their wings and search for mates with whom to pair off and begin new colonies.

Only a few will succeed. The rest will provide a huge seasonal feast for all kinds of waiting mouths: spiders and mantids, toads and monitor lizards, banded mongooses, jackals and bat-eared foxes. Swifts and nightjars gulp them down on the wing in their whiskered gapes. White storks born on the church towers of central Spain seek them on foot in the grass, and olive baboons scoop them up by the handful to stuff into their cheek pouches.

The storks are not the only migrants to appear. For weeks now large flocks of Caspian plovers – refugees from Russia's frozen steppes – have been flickering low over the plains, and pallid harriers have returned to range across the marshes farther west in the Mara Triangle, where more rain falls than on the drier central and eastern plains. European swallows, some fresh from southern English meadows, hawk for insects, swooping low over the broad backs of the Kichwa Tembo buffalo bulls, and black and white cuckoos from India skulk in the bushes along the Mara River.

Towards evening, in the last hour of daylight when the red-necked spurfowl begin to call, a lone cheetah rises from behind a clump of sodom apple bushes, stretches luxuriously with front legs extended and haunches raised, then begins to walk slowly across the grass.

The cheetah treads light and golden upon the plain. He is an old adult male, a

Above: Cheetahs are stalkers, specializing in high-speed chases in pursuit of Thomson's gazelles and impalas, which are their primary prey in the Serengeti-Mara. Male cheetahs hunting in twos or threes have been known to take animals up to the size of yearling wildebeest. Cheetahs hunt mainly during the daytime, thereby helping to avoid competition with other predators, particularly lions and hyenas. They occasionally hunt on moonlit nights.

stranger to the area, and he has not eaten. His belly is thin, drawn up tight beneath him in a graceful curve that complements his deep chest, long tail and swaybacked greyhound frame. His scabbed ears suggest that he might be suffering from sarcoptic mange, a skin disease spread by mites that make the host animal scratch constantly. But doing so can give rise to festering wounds which, in turn, may even lead to death through secondary infection. Such afflictions are not uncommon in lone male cheetahs, whose solitary lifestyle is more stressful than that of males who stay together.

After a few steps the scab-eared male slumps down again, yawns twice, revealing small canines and a pink tongue, and begins to groom himself, licking the creamy fur of his chest. Yet even at rest he never entirely relaxes his guard, lying on his side to hide from unfriendly eyes. His whole body language signals caution. As with all cheetahs, the art of concealment is second nature to him, and when he raises his head to stare through the grassheads with burning amber eyes he does not change his position.

Not all male cheetahs are loners. Most litter-mates stay together for life or join up with unrelated males to roam the plains in coalitions of twos and threes. Adult females, on the other hand, invariably lead solitary lives except when mating or accompanied by cubs. On the short-grass plains of the Serengeti National Park, where prey is migratory and absent for part of the year, they may wander across a home range as large as 1000 square kilometres. In the Masai Mara, which supports a greater abundance of year-round prey, home ranges are smaller and cheetahs more numerous.

The Mara's cheetah population appears to be stable at present and may even be increasing slowly, with between 30 and 40 present in the reserve from year to year and another 30 or so on the adjoining rangelands. Even so, the cheetah is by far the most endangered of Africa's three big cats. Although it occurs right across the Sahel from the Atlantic coast to the Horn of Africa and from Egypt down to Namibia and the Transvaal, its distribution is sparse and widely scattered, with no more than 15,000 to 20,000 animals throughout its entire range. Of these, about 800 live in Kenya.

Below: Male cheetah scent marking his territory. All cats spray urine tainted with scent from their anal glands against trees and bushes known as scent posts. These pungent chemical messages are long lasting, signalling whether the owner was male or female, mature or young, and when they last visited the area, helping to space individuals and avoid potentially dangerous encounters between rivals.

Previous page: Two of the Serena female's five-stong family of six-month-old cubs. Cheetahs are capable of running at speeds up to 112 kilometres per hour for short distances. They rarely pursue prey for more than 400-600 metres after which they stop to avoid heat stress, panting rapidly to lower their body temperature. As adults their claws are non-retractable, blunt and dog-like, helping to give them maximum purchase when running. They have a razor-sharp dew claw on the wrist which is used to snag and trip their prey.

Right: Cheetah cubs spend countless hours playing, particularly during the cooler hours, chasing after each other, wrestling and clambering up trees. This all helps to refine their hunting skills and to strengthen muscles.

For all cheetahs, life is fraught with danger. They lack the lion's overwhelming strength, the leopard's stocky physique and muscular power, the bone-crunching bite of the spotted hyena. Although similar in size to leopards, their jaws are small and they cannot fully retract their claws, which are blunt and dog-like with constant running. Females weigh about 40 kilograms and males 10 kilos more; the average lioness is twice as heavy. Even the cheetah's call – a high-pitched chirrup – sounds more like a bird than a major predator.

As daylight hunters, cheetahs may also be harassed by the safari vehicles that follow them across the plains in the hope of observing a kill. Even the presence of other cheetahs will sometimes cause them to run or melt away into the grass. In the Mara, where all the odds seem stacked against them, only constant alertness and fleetness of foot enable these beautiful spotted cats to coexist in the same rich hunting grounds as their more numerous and powerful enemies – the lion prides and hyena clans.

Above all, the cheetah relies on speed to stay alive for, unlike other predators, it does not scavenge but catches its own prey. It is the culmination of an ancient and inseparable bond between hunter and hunted. Over the millennia the cheetah has evolved stride by stride with the gazelles – the jinking, quicksilver pace of the one being matched by the elasticity and blistering acceleration of the other – to become the fastest animal on earth, capable of reaching 112 kilometres per hour. Every inch of its body – the flexible spine, sprinter's chest, small head and large nasal passages – has been fine-tuned for extra swiftness. In the precarious world of the cheetah every day is a race for life.

As the sun drops closer towards the horizon the old, lone cheetah rises to his feet and walks on across the plain. Groups of Thomson's gazelles that have been peacefully feeding unaware of his presence now look up as one, part to let him through, then follow in his wake as if hypnotized by his golden presence.

The cheetah ignores the nervously snorting Tommies. His eyes are fixed on a kongoni, or Coke's hartebeest, grazing beside its spindly-legged baby some little way off. As yet both mother and youngster are unaware of the approaching cat.

Tension crackles across the plain. The cheetah maintains his relentless advance. The kongoni continue to nibble at the grass. When their backs are turned the cat runs forward – half-crouching, with head held low – then hides behind a tuft of taller grass.

Suddenly he is up again and moving forward. The walk becomes a trot and, with no break in stride, the trot accelerates into a gallop. Too late the kongoni and its youngster explode away. The cheetah closes the distance between them in huge bounds, throwing up small puffs of dust every time his hind feet hit the ground.

Mother and baby jink as one, swerving this way and that to escape those pounding feet. At every turn the cheetah swerves with them, tail flung high in the air for balance, keeling over like a yacht in a stiff breeze. Desperately the mother turns again, but the cheetah is not watching her. Extending a slim foreleg, he sends the calf tumbling with a single side-swipe of his outstretched paw.

By the time the dust has drifted away the cheetah has throttled his victim while the mother kongoni can only watch helplessly from a distance. Hurriedly the cat begins to feed, looking around apprehensively between each mouthful – already the black shadows of vultures are drifting over the grass. As the birds drop towards him others see their fall to earth and follow, drawn in from far across the plains to form a swiftly descending vortex.

Spotted hyenas, which always follow the movements of vultures with intense interest, come loping from luggas and thickets in expectation of an easy meal. In no time the cheetah is forced to leave his hard-won kill as they move in, whooping and giggling

Left: Spotted hyenas are the most numerous of the Serengeti-Mara predators. They live in large clans and are highly adaptable, hunting singly or in groups. For many years they were thought to be purely scavengers, incapable of hunting for themselves — primarily because they are mainly active at night. Even a single hyena is capable of bringing down a full-grown wildebeest, though inevitably the commotion of the hunt soon attracts other hyenas to the scene. Hyenas do not employ a single killing bite, simply tearing their victim apart, killing it in the process of eating.

among the encircling vultures as more fall from the sky, landing with a rush of wings like the sound of shaken umbrellas.

The cheetah walks wearily away to the far side of the plain. There he stops to clean himself, licking his paws and then rubbing them over his bloodied muzzle. By now the sun has set. The few mouthfuls he gulped down before the scavengers arrived have not blunted his hunger and he will not hunt again before dawn. In the deepening dusk the enigmatic face with its characteristic black tear-stains appears more poignant than ever, but it is impossible to say what thoughts are passing through that small, round head.

Who is he, this solitary stranger? Where has he come from, and where will he go now? Is he the old male seen hunting earlier in the year on the plains near Rhino Ridge? In the Mara, no matter where he wanders, he will always face relentless competition from lions and hyenas, and the indignity he has suffered at Kichwa Tembo is a telling demonstration of just how hard the cheetah's life can be.

Beauty And Half-Tail

Chapter 3

December 3

Leopard Gorge

Out on the plains of the Masai Mara there is a feeling of the vastness of Africa, of open grasslands rising and falling like the waves of the sea, drawing the eye to the farthest horizon. And should you drive to that spot on the distant skyline you will find the same view repeated – more endless savannah rolling down to the Serengeti. But Leopard Gorge is different.

The gorge is steep-sided, walled about by stony ridges and tumbling granite rimrocks. Bush hyrax stare from its caves and crevices and, on either side, gnarled fig trees and euphorbias stand silhouetted against the sky, in places shutting out the early morning light when the plains below are already bathed in the sun's warming glow. At dusk it is an eerie spot, the haunt of eagle owls and Gabon nightjars; and even in the brightness of morning, when raucous parties of Rüppell's long-tailed starlings chatter in the treetops, there is a sense of being watched by unseen eyes.

A rough track runs down the middle of the gorge, worn by passing tyres of the endless stream of vehicles that come here every day. For, as its name suggests, this is a famous place for leopards. The female known as Beauty is here this morning, couched high in a monumental fig tree on the lip of the gorge. Beside her, wedged in a fork with head and legs dangling, is the carcass of a Thomson's gazelle she killed in the night. Leopards are not particularly large. A female is no more than one-third the size of a lioness but, pound for pound, they are the most powerful cats on earth. Although the gazelle must have weighed at least 22 kilograms – half as heavy as Beauty herself – she managed to haul it high into her larder-tree, where she has been feasting out of reach of lions and hyenas.

The gorge is an ideal refuge for leopards. In the Mara, to compete with lions and hyenas they must live wherever there is cover. One of the worst fates that can befall a leopard is to be caught out in the open with nowhere to hide. So they seldom stray far

Previous page: Fig Tree Ridge at sunset. This is prime leopard habitat, a maze of rocky hiding places and magnificent fig trees surrounded by acacia thickets providing access to prey such as impalas, gazelles, hares and hyrax. The ridge lies outside the reserve boundary so the animals here share the land with the Maasai and their livestock.

Right: Half-Tail's daughter, Beauty, at six months. From an early age leopards are expert climbers which is essential if they are to avoid conflict with dangerous competitors such as lions and hyenas. Beauty is the only survivor of Half-Tail's first litter of cubs. She was an extraordinarily trusting young leopard, comfortable in the presence of vehicles, just like her mother. When Half-Tail produced her next litter of cubs – Mang'aa and Taratibu – Beauty on occasion reunited briefly with her mother, even playing with the young cubs, confounding our image of leopards as highly solitary cats. Leopard females usually have cubs at two-year intervals; in this instance Beauty was only 14 months old when Half-Tail gave birth again, which could be why she continued to seek contact with her mother.

Above: Bush hyrax sunning themselves along Fig Tree Ridge. Hyrax are rabbit-sized mammals, sometimes referred to as rock rabbits. There are three species of hyrax in East Africa: bush hyrax, rock hyrax and tree hyrax. Bush hyrax are superb climbers, balancing on the thinnest branches to feed on leaves; rock hyrax eat mainly grass; tree hyrax browse or graze according to habitat. Hyrax are the closest living relative of the elephant, sharing a common ancestor dating back 40 million years. Young leopards stalk small creatures such as hyrax, hares and lizards from an early age, and by the time they are nine months old will almost certainly have made their first kill.

from the luggas and riverine forest edges. Rocks and caves and croton thickets, lairs of thorns, lofty trees – such is the leopard's secret world.

Secure in her tree Beauty dozes, although hers is the semi-sleep of cats. Her small round ears twitch constantly, sifting and deciphering the sounds that come to her on the morning breeze: the scolding voice of a grey-backed cameroptera, the deep-throated cooing of red-eyed doves, the distant whistle of a Maasai herdboy; and from time to time her eyes open – pale yellow discs with the pupils contracted to black pinpoints in the glare of the sun.

Seasonal movements of game scarcely touch her. Unlike lions, whose lives swing between glut and famine with the rhythms of the migration, Beauty can choose from an inexhaustible supply of smaller animals. Impala and Thomson's gazelles are her preferred prey, but she also catches hares, dik-diks, hyrax and guinea fowl – sometimes even jackals and African wild cats.

Later, when the day grows hotter and the sound of approaching safari vehicles echoes down the gorge, she will descend from her tree – pouring head first down its trunk like silk – to disappear into one of the narrow caves that have hidden generations of leopards before her. But for a while yet, having eaten her fill, she lies along an outspreading branch, indolently warming herself in the sun's first rays.

Leopards are the most adaptable and widely distributed of the world's big cats. They are found all over Africa, where they are equally at home in the rainforests of Zaïre as in the Namibian desert. In Kenya they even adopt the life-style of England's city-dwelling foxes, making night-time forays through the back gardens of suburban Nairobi.

Yet 20 years ago it was virtually impossible to find a leopard. Trophy hunters still shot them and ranch owners, who regarded them as a stock-raiding menace, put down bait laced with cattle dip as a cheap and deadly way of getting rid of them. But the biggest threat to Africa's leopards was the fortune to be earned from their beautiful spotted coats. During the 1960s and 1970s it was reported that as many as 70,000 were being killed every year to satisfy the fur trade's needs.

No wonder those that survived the poaching holocaust learned to shun human contact. Already solitary and largely nocturnal by nature, they became even shyer and more secretive in their habits. In those days it was possible to spend a month in the Mara without seeing a single leopard, and one fleeting glimpse of a spotted shadow melting away into the thickets was enough to become the highlight of any safari. Even the Serengeti's famous Seronera Valley struggled to maintain its reputation as the best place in East Africa to watch leopards. Nowhere was safe from the poachers.

The early 1970s brought a dramatic change in the leopard's fortunes. Suddenly it was no longer fashionable to wear leopard-skin coats, and, in 1975, all international trading in leopard and cheetah skins was banned. Two years later the Kenyan government announced a nationwide ban on the hunting of all wildlife, ending a system that had fallen into disrepute. Trophy hunting, like poaching, was by then completely out of hand, and Kenya's decision – reinforced by a further ban on the sale of wildlife products in curio shops – helped to ease the pressure on the leopard. But above all it was world opinion, fuelled by growing revulsion at the vanity and greed that could endanger an entire species, which probably saved the Mara's leopards.

In the Mara, where leopards have been fully protected for nearly two decades, numbers have steadily increased. At the same time a handful of individual leopards have learned to tolerate the presence of safari vehicles, rewarding visitors with intimate sightings undreamed of 20 years ago.

Yet the Mara leopards remain elusive because that has always been the best way for them to survive. Camouflaged in their spotted coats and moving mostly by night, they have learned to conduct nearly every aspect of their lives out of sight of human or animal eyes.

December 12

Fig Tree Ridge

It has often been said that baboons are a favourite prey of leopards. In the Mara, where easier prey is available, leopards tend to avoid them. True, the Mara leopards will sometimes hunt and kill baboons at night, or even pick off an individual by day if the opportunity arises. One of the surest indications that a cat is on the prowl is the male baboon's alarm call: a loud, gruff wah-hoo which is rapidly taken up the rest of the troop when danger threatens. But at other times it is the leopard that is at risk if cornered by the big adult males with their dog-like muzzles and huge canines.

This morning such a fate nearly befell Beauty's mother, Half-Tail. Already, earlier in her life, her tail had been bitten and torn by a baboon, eventually withering away to leave her with a lynx-like stump. Today she might even have lost her life.

She was resting curled up on the ground beside an acacia bush on Fig Tree Ridge, a ragged line of rocks and trees between Leopard Gorge and the road to Governor's Camp. She had already seen the baboon troop spreading out through the grass below to feed on shoots, seeds and acacia pods, but she must

Left: Half-Tail and Taratibu walking along Fig Tree Ridge. For the first eight weeks leopard cubs remain hidden, seeking the safety of caves and dense thickets. As they become more confident, cubs begin to follow their mother and she will lead them to the place where she has made a kill and stored it in a tree. Many leopard cubs do not survive, victims of attacks by lions, hyenas or even other leopards.

have felt they were far away enough for her to remain secure and undetected, for she lowered her head and appeared to doze.

She never saw the big male baboon detach himself from the rest of the troop and move in a nonchalant arc towards her. Clearly he had spotted her when she raised her head to stare across the plain. Closer he came, a menacing figure, stiff-legged and beady-eyed, muzzle thrust forward.

Half-Tail did not stir until the big baboon, hair bristling, ran the last few metres towards her. She must have heard his footfalls only at the very last moment, and there was a sudden blur of movement as she spun round to confront him. Then, for what seemed like an eternity but could only have been a few seconds, both animals stood there, face to face, canines bared in a terrifying display. The leopard hissed and coughed, and the baboon backed off without a sound. This time she was lucky. Had he barked in alarm it would have brought the whole troop to his defence and Half-Tail would have been fortunate to escape with a severe mauling.

Half-Tail is now nine years old and, being fairly approachable and easy to recognize, is probably the best-known leopard in the Mara. However, she was not the first to become accustomed to the presence of safari vehicles. That honour belonged to another female called Chui – Swahili for leopard – who was born in Leopard Gorge in 1978.

Four years later, in late 1982 or early 1983, Chui's mother produced another litter of twins, this time at Mara Buffalo Rocks, a massive stony outcrop with caves running through it; and six months later Chui produced a litter of her own in a cave on Fig Tree Ridge. Normally, leopard mothers move their cubs every so often to a new den to reduce the risk of discovery by predators. But drought had denuded the Mara of so much cover that the two families stayed put – attracting visitors from all over the world and enhancing the Mara's reputation for leopard viewing.

Early in 1984 Chui and her cubs vanished. By then Light and Dark, as the twins were known, were six months old and big enough to follow their mother. Months slipped by and still they did not reappear in their old haunts. Perhaps the pressure of so many vehicles had forced Chui to seek out new hiding places. But in October 1985, almost two years later, Chui was seen in Leopard Gorge with three new cubs, transferring them briefly to Fig Tree Ridge before disappearing again as mysteriously as she had arrived.

She was never seen again and her fate remains a mystery. For a while Leopard Gorge seemed strangely empty, but, in time, her place was taken by another leopard. The newcomer was known as the Paradise Female because she was born in 1987 in the Paradise area southeast of Governor's Camp. From there she had wandered north, then made her way up the Bila Shaka lugga to Leopard Gorge and Fig Tree Ridge, where she was observed mating with a huge, reclusive old male in February 1990.

The arrival of the Paradise Female was greeted with delight by the drivers who took tourists to Leopard Gorge, for she was even more tolerant of vehicles than Chui had been

Above: Male olive baboon. Male baboons can weigh up to 30 kilograms and are extremely powerful. They are armed with dagger-like canines up to 5 centimetres long, which they use to intimidate rivals and to defend themselves and fellow troop members against predators. In the Mara, leopards rarely prey on baboons, which have been known to seriously injure or even kill leopards. Staring is a threat among baboons and they flash their white eyelids in aggressive encounters with other baboons. Females make up the core of baboon society and remain in the troop in which they are born; males emigrate to a new troop as adolescents.

Left: Chui's six-month-old male cubs, Dark and Light, playing on Fig Tree Ridge in 1983. During the first six months leopard cubs spend a lot of time playing together, gradually spending more and more time on their own before eventually becoming independent during their second year. Young females often remain in the area in which they were born, overlapping part of their mother's home range. Male leopards do not form long-lasting bonds with individual females and play no part in raising their offspring, mating with females that are in season and then going their separate ways. But by defending a territory males help to prevent incursions by other males who might kill the cubs.

and would occasionally even rub her cheek against a Land Cruiser bumper or turn round and spray the wheels with her scent. When the long rains ended that year the Paradise Female was found with an impala kill stored in a tree on Emarti ya Faru; but she had lost her first litter of cubs – perhaps to lions or hyenas, or simply through inexperience.

That same year during the dry season the old male leopard that had mated with her in February attacked a Maasai herdboy who almost stumbled over the cat in its resting-place on the Ngorbop lugga. A dozen Maasai warriors gathered and flushed the leopard from its hiding place. The leopard charged, quick as lightning, badly mauling three of the warriors before it was finally speared to death.

It was around this time that the Paradise Female nearly lost her life when she was cornered by a troop of baboons. Two of the big males grabbed at her hind legs as she fled, causing her to falter. As other members of the troop piled in she flipped on her back to defend herself, hind legs pulled up and raking furiously with her claws. Somehow she managed to wriggle out from beneath the scrum and make good her escape, but during the struggle she was badly bitten and her tail was almost severed midway down. For days she dragged the remains after her, still attached by shreds of skin and flesh. Eventually they fell away and she acquired a new name from the safari drivers – Half-Tail. From now on she would be the most instantly recognizable of all the Mara leopards.

The following year Half-Tail was seen mating at Leopard Gorge with a new suitor – a young, dark male, not long independent, whose mother shared part of Half-Tail's range. The mating did not result in a litter, and within weeks of their encounter the young male met his end in a lopsided battle with lions of the Gorge Pride who surprised him in the open one morning as he was heading for the safety of the Ngorbop lugga.

Soon, however, Half-Tail was mated by the resident male whose territory overlapped her range and towards the end of 1992 she gave birth to three cubs on Fig Tree Ridge. Two were quickly lost to the lions, but the third, a female, survived. She became known as Beauty and, after the death of her two brothers, she was hurriedly moved to a new lair on the tree-lined Ngorbop lugga, which lies to the east of Bila Shaka lugga and winds its way down a shallow valley past the three rocky hillocks known as Malima Tatu. Despite constant harassment from baboons, the threat of lions and battles over food with ever-present hyenas, the lugga with its scattered trees and dense understorey of croton and acacia made an ideal home for Half-Tail and Beauty.

Beauty was an enchanting cub. She grew up among the inevitable throng of tourist vehicles attracted by her presence and would sometimes even creep beneath them, just as her mother had done in earlier years. Half-Tail herself still occasionally used them as a convenient blind when stalking prey. In all other respects Beauty was just like any other leopard cub – a natural tree climber, slinky smooth in her movements and insatiably curious, stalking small birds and agama lizards from an early age. By the time she was nine months old she had made her first kill, surprising a young hare crouched motionless in its form beneath the overgrown branches of a fallen acacia.

Without brothers or sisters to play with during the long hours when her mother went hunting, Beauty amused herself by flinging herself against the willowy stems of croton bushes or rolling pebbles along the bed of the lugga; when her mother returned she would leap all over her and the two of them would play together, tumbling, biting and grappling – always in fun and with claws sheathed – vital activity that would strengthen the young leopard's muscles, quicken her reflexes and refine the hunting skills she would need when the time came to fend for herself.

For Beauty, that time came much earlier than expected. Half-Tail had mated and become pregnant again when Beauty was barely one year old. There is usually a two-year interval between leopard litters – allowing time for cubs to grow up and become independent, usually when they are between between 18 months and two years old. But on this occasion her mother gave birth to a new litter of cubs when Beauty was only 14 months old.

Half-Tail's cubs were born on Fig Tree Ridge in November 1993, and what happened next provides a deeper insight into the leopard's secret world. By nature the leopard is a loner: it is truly the cat that walks by itself. But, as Beauty was to reveal, the leopard's social repertoire is much more flexible than was once believed.

On a number of occasions she was seen in the company of her younger siblings. Her presence was tolerated by their mother, though there were times when Half-Tail would hiss and growl to warn Beauty to keep her distance or to ensure that she did not play too roughly with the cubs. Eventually these encounters became more infrequent as Beauty adopted the solitary habits of adulthood, wandering eastwards from the upper end of Bila Shaka lugga but mainly staying south of the road to Narok.

Increasingly, as Beauty became harder to find, attention shifted to Half-Tail's new cubs. One was a male who became known as Mang'aa, Swahili for someone who doesn't care – a name that reflected his bold and confident nature. Mang'aa was totally relaxed in the presence of vehicles. He even began to view them as a source of protection, harmless objects as familiar as the sheltering rocks within whose caves and crevices he slept. When Mang'aa was frightened by the sight of lions or baboons or the distant sound of Maasai herdsmen he would sometimes seek refuge by keeping close to the cars, almost as if saying 'Try and get me now if you dare'.

Mang'aa's sister was named Taratibu, meaning gentle or careful. From an early age male cubs are noticeably bigger than female cubs, and by the time he was six months old Mang'aa could dominate his sister in disputes over food and was rougher when he played, making Taratibu bare her milk teeth and flatten her ears in protest.

Yet, despite the difference in size, the two cubs were inseparable during these first months of their lives, constantly engaged in play, sparring and cuffing each other with oversized paws. As they grew older, however, their bouts of play-fighting became shorter, brisker, more perfunctory. Increasingly they chose to spend time alone, often resting in different trees or under different bushes.

One day, when Mang'aa and Taratibu were eleven months old, Beauty made one of her irregular appearances in her mother's home range. She killed an impala and hung it in a tree, then called her young siblings, who were in the area, and allowed them to feed from the carcass. Once again, Beauty's behaviour revealed that the popular image of the leopard as a loner is an over-simplification of a lifestyle that is more complex than biologists first realized. However, leopards are generally intolerant over food and it was not long before Mang'aa became very aggressive and forced Taratibu to move aside and let him feed on his own. Meanwhile Beauty looked on, having already eaten her fill. Only when Mang'aa was also full did he allow Taratibu to return.

Sadly, this was almost the last time that Taratibu was seen alive. A month later, early one morning and almost a year to the day after the cubs were born, she was found lying dead on the ground. Nearby lay the scar-faced lioness that had killed her, watched by two male lions from farther off. Mang'aa, too, was watching from the top of a tree where he had been feeding on the carcass of a Thomson's gazelle; and in another tree some 40 metres from the scene was Half-Tail, Taratibu's mother, her stump twitching in distress.

As is so often the case when this happens, Taratibu had not been eaten by the lions. Had she been killed by hyenas they would have finished off her entire carcass — flesh, bones, fur and all. But the lions had killed the young leopard simply because she was a competitor within their territory who could not be tolerated.

Mang'aa continued to be seen with Half-Tail until the end of the long rains in May 1995, when he was a year and a half old. Although he was killing for himself by this age, he sometimes still fed from prey brought down by his mother. But, as the year went by and he became completely independent, he began to wander between the network of luggas that break up the acacia country between Musiara gate and the road to Narok. For the time being this is Mang'aa's territory, although now and then he simply disappears among the littered boulders and dense acacia scrub to the north of Fig Tree Ridge.

Half-Tail, meanwhile, freed from her parental duties, was seen mating with a handsome new male during August. In mid-October — the next time she was in oestrus — she was again seen mating, this time on one of the Malima Tatu hills. If she is pregnant her new cubs should be born some time in January 1996.

As for Beauty, she now is far shyer of vehicles than when she was a cub. Too often she was harassed by poorly trained drivers who, urged on by clients eager for a dramatic photograph, pressed ever closer, denying her the space she needed. At first she would just hiss and snarl. Later, provoked beyond endurance, she took to charging at cars in an attempt to force them to leave. Now when she hears a vehicle approaching she often just melts away into thick cover or slinks off along the rocky rim of Leopard Gorge.

Previous page: Half-Tail stalking through red-oat grass near the northern end of the Ngorbop lugga. Leopards are the most adaptable of all of the big cats and there are far more leopards in Africa than lions or cheetahs, but due to their secretive habits they are less often seen. Although much of their hunting takes place during the hours of darkness, leopards also hunt in the daylight, particularly when they have cubs to feed and must kill more frequently. During the rains the Mara's tall stands of red-oat grass engulf predators in a cloak of grass making hunting in the day much easier.

Right: Maasai warriors dancing after having had their hair shaved off during the eunoto ceremony that marks the transition from warrior to junior elder. The Maasai have always lived side by side with the wild animals, relying on their cattle for their needs — food, bedding, dung to plaster their houses, and as wealth and status. Consequently many of East Africa's finest wildlife areas are found in Masailand, such as Masai Mara and Amboseli in Kenya, and Serengeti and Ngorongoro Crater in Tanzania.

Alone Against The Wild

Chapter 4

January I

Mara Triangle

The New Year has begun with the Mara looking as green as Ireland. Last week it rained heavily for three days, and vast areas of the plains between Serena Hill and the anti-poaching guardpost at Ngiro Are are now carpeted with new grass.

It rained again during the night, creating a magical dawn with layers of mist hanging over Kichwa Tembo Plain while the escarpment above lay bathed in sunlight. Although the storm seems to have passed the horizons are still piled high with cliffs of cloud, giving the huge apocalyptic skies that are typical of the Mara at this time of year. The light is stupendous, dazzling one minute, dark and brooding the next, and wherever you look there is life.

In hollows where pools of rainwater have collected small groups of sacred ibis and open-billed storks are feeding. Montagu's harriers sail low across the grass, following every rise and fall of the plain on their long, buoyant wings, and parties of European swallows hawk for insects between the Balanites trees that give these landscapes of the Mara Triangle such a pleasing, park-like appearance.

A sweep of the binoculars reveals herds of impala, some a hundred strong, the males duelling furiously with horns low to the ground. In the distance a herd of elephants is on the move – ghostly shadows in the mist with just the faintest gleam of tusks. Elsewhere, shafts of sunlight pick out troops of olive baboons, scattered groups of zebra and kongoni, a magnificent bull eland with 20 cows – and a solitary lioness under a tree.

Only when the lioness stands up and moves away does it become apparent that other eyes have been watching her. From beneath another Balanites tree some 400 metres distant a wary mother cheetah is slinking away in the opposite direction followed by her five half-grown cubs. When the lioness has disappeared over the rise the cheetah lies down and chirrups to her cubs, which huddle together between her outstretched legs, attempting to suckle. But their mother's milk has long since dried up as young cheetahs are fully weaned at three months and these cubs are now eight months old. Nevertheless, socializing in this way with their mother must give them a certain sense of comfort and underlines their dependence on her.

A cheetah's life is fraught with difficulties, but for this mother and her large litter it must be unduly hard. Having five extra mouths to feed has altered her habits. Now when she hunts she concentrates on adult gazelles rather than the easier but smaller meals provided by fawns and hares. Even so, she herself has less to eat, as is evident from her thin belly.

To add to her problems, whenever she spots a group of gazelles and begins to move towards them the cubs try to follow, often spoiling the hunt. In open country it is difficult enough for a single cheetah to stalk unseen. With five playful youngsters in tow it must be almost impossible.

Previous page: Occasionally during the rainy season the dawn is shrouded in a blanket of mist which cloaks the valleys and riverine forests in white. There are two rainy seasons each year: the short rains of mid-October through to early January and the long rains of April, May and June.

Above: Female impalas live in herds of between 10 and 50 individuals, wandering over a large home range and passing through a number of male territories as they search for food. They do not stay permanently on the territory of a single male. During the dry season very large herds of females and males, of up to 200 individuals may occur. Impalas are mixed feeders, taking short green grass during the rains, and browsing on the leaves and seed pods of bushes during the dry season. They prefer to drink daily.

Already, however, they are beginning to learn the skills they will need to survive on their own. Every so often when their mother lifts her head in a certain way they respond by stopping their play for a while. And it is at this time of their lives that she catches and releases gazelle fawns so that they can practise the vital art of killing for themselves.

On one occasion the mother tried to stalk a bachelor group of eight Thomson's gazelles which were lying in a circle. Nearby stood four Grant's gazelles – larger and paler than the Tommies and with white rumps extending above the tail. Whenever the Tommies looked up she would freeze until they began feeding again and she could continue to creep up on them. Then one of the Grant's snorted, and at once all the Tommies were on

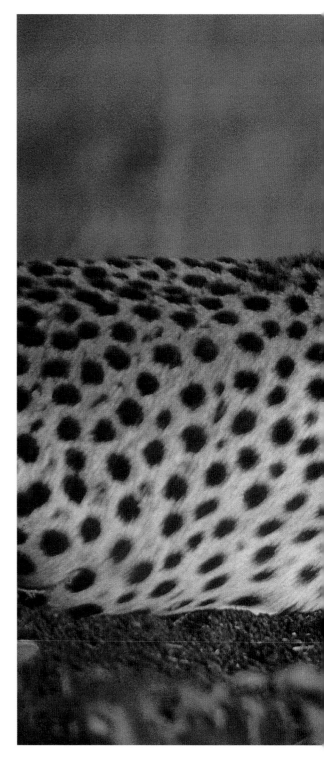

Right: Cheetahs produce larger litters of cubs than the other big cats – up to eight have been recorded though the more usual number is three to five cubs. Many cubs are killed by lions and hyenas as well as a host of other smaller predators, such as eagles, secretary birds, small cats and the larger mongooses. Cubs start to follow their mother when they are six weeks old, and have a mantle of long white hair along their neck and back which disappears when they are three months old.

their feet and running towards her – almost as if taunting the cheetah for having lost the element of surprise.

After this latest failure mother and cubs moved off to seek the shade and stayed there for the rest of the day. When evening came and the family had roused itself from its long siesta, the mother stood up and moved off towards higher ground, the youngsters bounding after her, stalking and leaping over each other as they went.

In their procession across the plain they surprised Caspian plovers standing motionless in the grass. Male widow birds in full breeding plumage fluttered overhead, trailing their absurdly long tail feathers. Fifteen banded mongooses rippled across the ground from one termite mound to the next and warthogs trotted away over the skyline with strings of tiny piglets following as fast as their legs would carry them.

The cheetahs came to a dead tree which had been knocked over by elephants; and here, while the mother rested and kept watch, her family scampered and romped. For 20 minutes they played king-of-the-castle on the sloping trunk, swinging their

Left: Male red-collared widow bird displaying itself prominently on a bush. Male widow birds are transformed during the breeding season, moulting their drab sparrow-like plumage, becoming more colourful and growing long tail feathers as a way of attracting females. When not in breeding plumage males resemble females.

Below: Male warthog. Warthogs are an important resident prey species for the Mara's predators – particularly for the lions and leopards. Hyenas and cheetahs sometimes also take young warthogs. Lions will at times dig warthogs out of their burrows. Both males and females have wart-like protuberances below their eyes and on the sides of their faces, which may help to protect them from injury when fighting with their tusks. They live and breed in old termite mounds, commandeering the burrows created by aardvarks. They prefer to feed on short green grass, and use their disc-like snouts and heavy upper tusks for rooting among tussocks and digging out roots, tubers and bulbs. When threatened they head for the nearest burrow, reversing down the hole to protect themselves from attack. They are active during the day and sleep in burrows at night.

long tails to balance themselves. When they grow older they will use fallen trees and termite mounds as vantage points from which to look for prey, but they will never become true climbers like leopards. They lack the razor-sharp claws and natural agility that allow the leopard to feel truly at home in the tallest tree.

When tired of play they crouched at the edge of a pool and five pink tongues lapped at the water until thirst was satisfied. Then the mother resumed her journey, leading her cubs towards a broad green slope covered with groups of zebras and topi. Where the slope ended in a long ridge hundreds of Thomson's gazelles and their tiny, bouncing fawns had gathered, drawn to the high ground by the sudden flush of fresh young grass.

Behind them the western sky turned red, picking out the gazelles and their fawns in sharp silhouette. A whole day had passed and still the cheetahs had not fed. Now, as the shadows began to lengthen, there would be one last chance to hunt and kill before nightfall.

January 3

Bila Shaka Lugga

A solitary black rhino has been seen browsing among the acacia thickets of Bila Shaka lugga. It is the same young male that first appeared in September, and his arrival has caused great excitement. He is the first rhino to appear in the northern Mara since 1990.

The Mara rhinos are not often found in the open. They prefer the sanctuary of the luggas, the dappled tunnels under the croton bushes and the dry stony places where the wait-a-bit thorn spreads its fish-hook barricades. But sometimes this young male wanders out into the plains country – where he was also spotted browsing this morning, drawn by an abundance of the acacia seedlings and leguminous herbs that are much favoured by rhinos.

Unlike the free-wheeling zebras and wildebeest, he stood heavy and foursquare on the plain as if rooted to the spot, a dull-witted dreadnought from an earlier epoch when dinosaurs roamed the earth, plucking leaves and shoots with his prehensile upper lip. Red-billed oxpeckers rode on his back, feeding on the ticks embedded in his iron-grey hide. Sometimes they probed into ears and nostrils, but he seemed oblivious to their fluttering presence. The association of bird and rhino is a perfect example of symbiosis – for the oxpeckers the rhino is a walking banquet of nourishing parasites; in return, the birds' sharp eyes and noisy alarm calls warn him if danger threatens.

With its great horned head and lizard-lidded eyes the rhino is a prehistoric, almost mythical creature, a relict beast whose ancestors have walked the earth for 60 million years. Recently, however, the black rhino has come perilously close to the end of the trail. Twenty years ago there were perhaps 65,000 in Africa. Today, after two decades of relentless poaching, fewer than 3000 have survived.

In the 1950s the Mara was home to as many as 200 rhinos. But poaching, together

Above: A cow rhino usually keeps her calf hidden during the first few weeks to try and avoid predation by lions and hyenas. During the last thirty-five years 60,000 black rhino have been slaughtered in Africa for their horns: carved into dagger handles in the Yemen and used in traditional medicine in the Far East. Only 2500 black rhino survive today. This female and her month-old calf were photographed in the Ngorongoro Crater, in Tanzania, which, like the Mara, still provides a refuge for free-ranging black rhino.

with a huge decline in their favoured croton thickets caused by grass fires and elephant damage, took a heavy toll. By 1972 the Mara population had been whittled down to 108 rhinos. And still the poachers came – until ten years later there were just 11 left. In the Mara, as elsewhere in Kenya and, indeed, throughout Africa, the future of the black rhino now hung in the balance.

In 1983, in a final bid to stop the poaching and save the Mara's last rhinos from extinction, a special team of local rangers was put into the field. Money was raised by Friends of Conservation – a wildlife charity established by Abercrombie & Kent, one of Africa's best-known safari companies – and the project rolled into action.

Today, 14 years later, the Masai Mara black rhino surveillance and monitoring programme is acknowledged as one of Kenya's greatest success stories. The poaching was halted and rhino numbers have more than trebled, from 11 to 39, making this the largest free-ranging black rhino population in East Africa. A further 20 or so animals live in the Loita forest east of the reserve.

Previous page: A pack of banded mongooses standing alert in response to a predator. Banded mongooses are active during the daytime and live in packs of 5–30 individuals; each pack defending a territory. They are often seen around termite mounds, which provide them with a safe refuge, a breeding site and a comfortable place to sleep. A number of males and females breed in each pack and all pack members help to guard and feed the young; there is no dominant pair. Pack members forage for insects such as beetles, grasshoppers, crickets, millipedes, termites, grubs and snails, and will also feast on reptiles, birds' eggs, nestlings and small mammals. Hard-shelled items like eggs, snails and millipedes are hurled backwards between the legs to smash them open against a rock or tree.

All this is a far cry from the dark days of 1981, when only one rhino was seen regularly in the northern Mara. Her name was Halima and she was usually to be found in the area aptly known as Rhino Ridge. Poachers had killed her mother in 1978, but by then Halima was old enough to fend for herself.

Everyone knew Halima. She was unusually placid and, like all rhinos, a creature of habit, staying within a home range of about 15 square kilometres that provided her with browse, water, favourite places in which to dust-bathe and wallow and, from time to time, a mate in the formidable shape of Kioko, one of the Mara's last surviving rhino bulls.

In 1981 Halima was shot in the shoulder by poachers but recovered after having the bullet removed. Over the next nine years she produced three calves, the first of which was killed by lions on Rhino Ridge. When it seemed that the second calf would meet a similar fate, mother and child were captured and moved to an oxbow on the Mara River. There, it was thought, they would be safer, but the Marsh Lions came in the night and mauled Halima's baby. Next morning the wounded calf was captured and flown to Nairobi, where it was cared for by Daphne Sheldrick, an expert at raising wild orphans, and later released in Nairobi National Park.

In 1988 Halima produced her third calf – and again the lions ambushed it, pressing home their attack with such determination that rangers were forced to shoot some of them to protect the infant rhino.

Then, in April 1990, Halima herself was found dead. She had been shot at point-blank range and her horns cut off. But who killed her? If it was poachers, why did they abandon the horns in the grass just a few metres from the body? These would have been worth tens of thousands of dollars when carved into ornate dagger handles in North Yemen or ground into medicinal powder in the Far East. One theory is that she was killed by someone with a grudge against the authorities. If so, it was a cruel revenge on a gentle creature whose presence had delighted thousands of visitors.

Now, after an interval of six years, the rhino seen this morning has taken her place. He is young yet, but already he is heavier than an adult buffalo and his huge, ponderous presence, drifting like a sleep-walker through the acacia bushes, fills a gap that has been here too long.

January 5

Kichwa Tembo

At last the long-awaited clash between the Kichwa Tembo lions and their nomadic rivals has taken place. For days the two brothers served notice of their claim to Kichwa Tembo Plain, gouging deep scratch marks in the ground with their hind feet, spraying bushes with their unmistakable pungence and responding in kind to the thunderous voices of the pride males.

In the end the struggle was furious but short-lived. At first the two black-maned Kichwa Tembo males stood their ground as the nomads ran towards them. But, when the two pairs of lions met – colliding in a rumbling wall of muscle, teeth and claws – one of the two veterans turned and fled for his life.

There was no such easy escape for his companion. Isolated and outnumbered, he rolled on his back with hind legs bunched to protect his rear, signalling submission. But the brothers were not finished yet. They tore into him, causing him to lash out in pain and rake one of his assailants across the face. Then, somehow, he managed to extricate himself from the writhing, snarling melee and hobble off after his companion. His tormentors followed for a while, heavy manes swinging as they trotted across the plain. When he disappeared into the Sabaringo lugga and emerged on the far side, still limping, they stopped and roared after him as if to say 'Don't come back'.

Defeat for the Kichwa Tembo males means a return to the forgotten hardships of life beyond the pride. If they are lucky they may form a new alliance with one or more nomadic males and make a bid for a new territory. But age is not on their side.

Male lions lead glorious but brief lives – maybe 12 years at best. In their prime as pride-masters they are truly the lords of the plains, but their fall from grace is tragic to behold. Without lionesses to kill for them their condition deteriorates as they are forced to hunt and scavenge for themselves. As outcasts even their luxuriant manes have outlived their purpose. They may serve to intimidate other males, but a full-grown mane also makes it much harder to stalk undetected through the long grass to within charging distance of zebra or wildebeest.

Eventually, as these old warriors become thinner and hungrier the parasites that permanently infest their bodies grow stronger and more numerous. Weakness and ill-health become a vicious circle and, as often as not, one that ends with ignominy in the jaws of hyenas.

For victorious nomads, however, it is a different story. When the Kichwa Tembo males had finally disappeared from sight the two brothers turned away. One walked to a nearby bush, sniffing with interest before swinging around with tail arched high to drench it with a stream of urine. Mixed with secretions from his anal glands its pungent odour will linger for days, a powerful message that other lions would be foolish to ignore. Then the brothers came together, rubbed their huge, bearded faces against each other and settled down – nomads no longer, but the new lords of Kichwa Tembo.

January 11

Mara Serena Hill

The three Serena pride males have fared better than their two former companions who have just been exiled from the Kichwa Tembo pride. Since this trio left Kichwa Tembo more than six months ago they have remained firmly in control of the Serena territory, where they consort with the two Serena lionesses and their three sub-adult youngsters.

Two of the males were patrolling around Serena Hill early this morning, scraping and scent-marking as if in response to the roars of the Paradise pride across the river. One has a huge black mane and tufts of hair sprouting from his elbows, and his companion has a distinct, brown beard. In addition, Black Mane has a split nostril, perhaps the result of some forgotten squabble over food when he was younger. Brown Beard, too, has been in the wars, but his wounds are more recent. There is an ugly open wound on his forehead with flies clustered around it. Despite their scars, however, the Serena pride males are acknowledged to be the finest in the Mara.

When they both disappeared into an extensive patch of croton bush Black Mane was the first to emerge on the other side, where he lay down and waited for his companion. As they moved on into the open, walking one behind the other, Black Mane roared – and zebra and topi hurried over the rise of the hill, pausing on the skyline as if spellbound by the great beasts sauntering past.

January 14

Kampi ya Fisi

One of the great joys of observing lions for any length of time is learning to recognize individual animals. The pride males are usually the easiest to identify, especially if, like Scruffy, the Ol Kiombo male, they have a distinctive mane. Others have prominent scars or torn ears, and every lion has its own unique pattern of whisker spots. The same is true of leopards. Half-Tail, of course, is easy to recognize – but even if her hindquarters are hidden she has a distinctive black spot on her pink nose just above the right nostril. In no time individuals like Half-Tail can become as familiar as old friends. Having entered their world and been so close to them, it is impossible not to become bound up with their lives and wonder what they are doing when you are far away.

Left: Scruffy, one of the Ol Kiombo pride males. Not all males develop fine manes, and in the desert areas of northern Kenya some of the males never grow proper manes. To be successful as a pride male and sire cubs it is essential to form a coalition, usually with close relatives – brothers or cousins. Strength is in numbers, and the larger coalitions are generally the most successful in siring offspring.

But the pleasure of knowing them so well makes it all the more distressing when they die. Today, out of the blue, came news that a leopard has been killed by seven lions of the Kampi ya Fisi pride. Apparently it was cornered in the acacia bush country north of the Narok road, not far from the Mara River Safari Camp.

No one has been able to identify the leopard except to say that it was a young male, and the fear is that it could be Half-Tail's son, Mang'aa. If so, it means that both cubs from Half-Tail's last litter have been killed by lions, demonstrating yet again the perils of being a leopard in lion country.

January 17

Kampi ya Fisi

The sight of a cheetah never fails to quicken the heart. Although not uncommon in the Mara, they are less numerous than leopards and roam so widely as to be difficult to find at times. Early morning, when they are still active, is usually the best time to look. As the day grows hotter they retire into the shade, crawling beneath the outspread branches of an acacia bush where they are impossible to see in the shadows. But at this early hour, armed with binoculars, one may be lucky enough to pick out the familiar triangular outline of a cheetah sitting upright on a distant ridge.

Too often, what appears at first glance to be a cat silhouetted against the sunlit grasslands turns out to be a tree stump or a boulder, or even a gazelle feeding, head down, at a deceptive angle. But persistence and a knowledge of the bush eventually bring their rewards.

As with all predators an understanding of the behaviour of prey animals is an invaluable aid to locating cheetahs, and so it was this morning. Two hours of searching had produced the impressive spectacle of a dozen lions, members of the Kampi ya Fisi pride, tearing at a zebra kill in the heart of the extensive croton thicket that lies close to the Narok road beyond Leopard Gorge. The safari drivers call this thicket the 'military camp' because, they say, it is always guarded by an army of lions!

But of cheetahs there was no sign. The first hour of light, the best time to hunt while the air is still cool, was long past. Now, like the Kampi ya Fisi lions, it was better to seek the shade. Only the Thomson's gazelles seemed oblivious to the sun's fierce glare. Unlike the impalas, which huddled together in pools of shadow at the edges of thorn thickets, the Tommies remained far out on the open plains, grazing calmly in small herds.

Suddenly, as if at an unseen signal, one group stopped feeding. Their heads went up, and next moment they were off, black side-stripes flashing. Some ran, bouncing stiff-legged over the plain in the gait known as 'stotting' or 'pronking' – a sure sign of predators on the prowl – then stopped and stared intently in the direction from which they had just fled. Moments later cheetahs came walking boldly over the horizon. All surprise lost, they no longer bothered to conceal themselves but continued their journey over the plain in full view of the watching gazelles, which now turned and fell in behind them as if hypnotized by the presence of the two swift cats.

After a while the cheetahs sat down and began to groom each other, rubbing cheeks and licking the thick spotted fur around neck and shoulder. Then the smaller of the two lay down and rolled on her back, inviting her brother to play – which he did, cuffing and nuzzling between her flailing paws.

These fellow travellers of the high plains are litter-mates, perhaps 15 months old and not long independent of their mother. In these first months of freedom they still take comfort in each other's presence. Later, when the female left her brother to lie in the shade some distance off, he called after her with a pathetic chirrup, as if discomforted to find himself on his own, then rejoined her for another bout of cheek-rubbing and purring before they both settled down to sleep.

It rained briefly in the afternoon, but the sun came out again before evening, lighting up the green plains and making them stand out in vivid contrast to the departing storm clouds. Now every horizon was pricked by the horned heads of Thomson's gazelles. The cheetahs watched them with renewed interest, then yawned, stretched luxuriously and walked out into the shining grass.

Their first hunting foray was a disaster, and it soon became apparent that the male is an inept and clumsy hunter. He was too eager, rushing in before the pair of them had stalked close enough to launch a successful attack on the gazelles, which were easily able to outrun him. As is often the case with young cheetahs his sister seems altogether sharper and more grown up. She ignored the adult gazelles – which had stopped, snorting and twitching, to watch from a safe distance – and began to search the ground purposefully.

Almost immediately a gazelle fawn popped up from its hiding place where it had been lying, chin to the earth. Both cheetahs immediately gave chase, but it was the female who quickly closed the gap and sent it spinning through the air.

She dropped the fawn as her brother joined her. For a minute the pair just stood there, panting heavily and looking nervously around for the scavengers that so often deprive them of their kills. This time they were lucky. The female carried the limp body under a bush where they would not be seen. Her brother followed, and together they fed hurriedly and without rancour, consuming their meal so quickly that 20 minutes later when the sun slid behind the Isuria escarpment there was nothing left.

Afterwards both cats groomed themselves. The female licked the blood from her brother's muzzle, who purred noisily with contentment. Then the pair of them rose and wandered off into the gathering darkness.

It is touching to see their attachment to each other, and for a while yet the brother will find solace in his sister's company. No doubt she will continue to be the more effective hunter,

Left: Cheetah females often catch young prey animals such as this Thomson's gazelle fawn and then release them to allow their cubs to practise their hunting skills. Though all young cats instinctively know how to stalk and pounce, it takes time for them to perfect the killing bite that big cats use to strangle their prey. Even when they become independent between 14 and 18 months, young cheetahs are still rather clumsy hunters.

catching hares and sniffing out Thomson's gazelle fawns, her favourite prey, until both of them develop the speed and cunning that will enable them to catch adult gazelles. However, as soon as she becomes sexually receptive for the first time at the age of about 22 months she will attract a mate – who will drive her brother away and may even try to kill him.

The young male seems strangely unsuited for the reclusive life that will almost certainly be his unless, as sometimes happens, he pairs up with another young male. Mostly, though, such coalitions of male cheetahs are formed by litter-mates. These are the fortunate ones, who may stay together for the rest of their lives. A coalition finds strength in numbers, its members hunting together and eventually claiming a territory of their own where they can seize every opportunity to mate with passing females.

Very different is the lonely life which the young male cheetah can expect in a few months' time. Then, his sister gone, he must fend for himself. Never again will his coat be so thick and glossy. He must be on his guard from dawn to dusk, not only to avoid the lions and spotted hyenas which are the cheetah's constant enemies but also to prevent other male cheetahs from finding and killing him on his lonely wanderings across the Mara.

Kingdoms Of The Grass

Chapter 5

February 3

Gol Kopjes, Serengeti

Out in the vastness of the Serengeti a cow wildebeest lies down in the grass to calve. For eight and a half months she has carried her youngster inside her. Together they made the great journey west and then north, following the promise of rain towards the dry-season feeding grounds of the Masai Mara. Somehow she managed to avoid the jaws of the giant Grumeti crocodiles and emerged unscathed from the mad stampedes that drowned so many of her kind along the Mara River.

Day after day in the Mara she listened to the pride males roaring, and her nights were filled by the insane giggling of hyenas squabbling over kills. But between the moments of sudden danger she fed peacefully, chomping methodically at the close-bitten turf with the rest of the herd.

When the grass was exhausted they moved on. Backwards and forwards across the Mara they wandered, seeking out the greenest places until, in late October, the imminent rains beckoned them south once more − a monstrous army, more than one million strong, streaming away in winding columns as far as the eye could see.

After leaving the Mara, the herds worked their way steadily down from the Serengeti's northern woodlands towards the southernmost limits of their range, their journey eased by the onset of the rains. By December they had crossed the Seronera River, where they tarried awhile, eating their way across the red-oat grasslands. Then, harassed by lion prides, watched by the Seronera leopards, followed by loping clans of spotted hyenas, they marched on − pouring south like a black tide around the Simba Kopjes, the granite outcrops that tower 30 metres above the road to Naabi gate.

The last, scattered trees were now far behind them. Ahead lay nothing but an infinity of grass, pierced in places by the wind-worn boulders of the Gol Kopjes; and, as the blue

Previous page: Gol Kopjes. The word kopje is a Dutch word meaning 'little head'. These beautiful granite outcrops, or inselbergs, are part of the ancient heart of Africa underlying the Serengeti plains, some of which are 600 million years old. In fact some of the oldest rocks in the world − three billion years old − are to found near Seronera in the centre of the Serengeti park. The kopjes are a haven for leopards and lions, owls and eagles, hyrax and agama lizards, as well as providing the wandering herds with pools of rainwater and seepage from springs to drink from.

Right: Wildebeest calves are on their feet within five minutes of birth − faster than any other ungulate − and can soon run as fast as the adults. More than 400,000 calves are born each year on the Serengeti's short grass plains, the majority within a few weeks in February and March. The sheer volume of calves swamps the predators with food − survival is in being born among such vast numbers. This peak in births is due to the synchronized rutting of the bull wildebeest in June at the beginning of the dry season, when the herds are leaving the plains and are at their most concentrated.

outlines of the Ngorongoro Highlands drew closer, the wildebeest at the head of the columns began to run as if glad to be back on the short-grass plains they had last seen more than six months before. If the migration has a beginning it is surely here, at the time of birth in the southern Serengeti. The life of the wildebeest is an endless journey, following the thunder in search of rain and grass. But, at the turning of the year, they are always drawn back to these ancestral calving grounds.

All through January their numbers swelled with new arrivals until the plains were black to the limits of vision. Here they moved back and forth between the Gol Mountains and the Moru Kopjes, settling briefly wherever the sporadic rains coaxed a fresh flush of grass into life. Sometimes the herds wandered outside the park as far as the Salei Plains beyond the Gol Mountains and to Olduvai Gorge, the most famous archaeological site in Africa. Here, as well as the fossil skulls of man's first ancestors, wildebeest bones have been unearthed – proof that the Serengeti herds have roamed these plains for at least a million years.

A week ago the greatest numbers of wildebeest were massed near Lake Lagarja, a soda lake whose saline shallows they crossed frequently, wading hock deep on their way from one grazing area to another. Now they are spread among the Gol Kopjes, some 20 kilometres farther north, and the pregnant cow is with them.

Other cows watch as she lies on her side, thin legs outstretched, her swollen body convulsed with the contractions that have already forced the head and forelegs of the foetus to appear. Her eyes roll – then her teeth are bared in pain as she struggles to her feet and, in the very moment of rising, drops her calf in the grass.

The mother turns to lick the wet, glistening bundle, which is already jerking its spindly legs. Within five minutes the little bull-calf has staggered to his feet and a minute later is sufficiently mobile to find his mother's teats. Two weeks from now he should be able to run as fast as any wildebeest on the plains.

The moments immediately after birth are critical as it is then that by sound, smell and taste the mother and her baby are imprinted in each other's memory. Never again will the young calf be quite so vulnerable. If a predator appeared on the scene, causing the pair to become separated before imprinting had taken place, he would almost certainly be doomed. Lost infants are not uncommon on the plains and are a pathetic sight. In their search for their mothers they may approach anything that moves – sometimes even walking right up to a lion or hyena.

Ironically, this youngster's greatest chance of avoiding predators is the arrival of thousands of others like him across the short-grass plains. Calving, which began in late January, will continue until March, with 80 per cent of all wildebeest mothers giving birth within the same three weeks. As a stratagem for survival it is crude but effective. Quite simply, the avalanche of births produces such a glut of calves that the predators cannot possibly eat them all.

With its long Roman nose and doleful expression the wildebeest is the strangest of antelopes. Nature has given it the head of an ox, the mane of a horse and the sloping hindquarters of a hyena. It is the clown of the plains, liable at any moment to go prancing madly over the grass for no apparent reason, supported on absurdly thin-looking legs that hide unbelievable powers of endurance. Yet, judging by the sheer numbers now massed on the calving grounds, the wildebeest is also the most successful animal on the savannah.

February 15

Naabi Hill, Serengeti

Naabi Hill is a prominent landmark that guards the main entrance to Serengeti National Park. Every vehicle entering the park must stop here and be registered with the authorities before heading north along the road to Seronera.

Until December the plains around Naabi Hill were a desolation of dust and stubble. There is no permanent water here and, apart from an occasional ostrich or Grant's gazelle, no visible sign of life. Dust devils driven by hot, dry winds come boiling over the barren ridges and cruel mirages transform the faraway summits of the Itonjo Hills into islands floating above a dream of blue water. But how different it is once the rains have cast their spell.

The short-grass plains spring to life, the sweet turf greener than an English meadow. In the cold, bright mornings they shine with dew, and from every direction comes the gleam of water held in natural hollows and depressions. Each waterhole mirrors the reflections of zebra and wildebeest and the dawns are filled with rushing wings as flights of doves and yellow-throated sandgrouse stream in to drink. At such times there is nowhere in the world more beautiful than these wide Tanzanian plains.

One of their most striking features is the almost total absence of trees. Elsewhere in the Serengeti open grasslands have evolved as the result of endless cycles of fire and grazing. Here, however, they predominate because of the presence of a hard-pan just beneath the surface which prevents trees and other deep-rooted woody plants from gaining a foothold. The result is a carpet of short green grass that plays a vital role in the lives of the wildebeest and zebra. Spreading out around Naabi in every direction it covers 10,000 square kilometres of the Serengeti and adjacent Ngorongoro Conservation Area and is the hub around which the whole migratory cycle revolves.

Here the dominant grasses are very different from the waving, waist-high meadows to the north. Short-stemmed and shallow-rooted, they spring from soils of wind-blown volcanic ash spewed out by the long-dead craters of the Ngorongoro Highlands. Consequently they are rich in minerals essential for healthy growth – potassium, sodium and calcium – giving every newborn wildebeest the best possible start in life and providing rich pastures for the lactating females.

Longer grasses appear farther north and west, where the annual rainfall increases and the soil changes. First there is a belt of intermediate species: drop-seed and blue-stem. Then come the first waves of the beautiful red-oat grass, Themeda triandra, with its three-fingered tassels, which covers much of the Seronera Valley and its black cotton soils. Other species include Rhodes grass, star grass, various species of the tall thatch grass, Hyparrhenia, and the highly unpalatable wire grass, Pennisetum insculpta, which is ignored by most grazers and stands in ragged clumps above the nibbled sward.

As the dry season advances the longer grasses set their seed and the dying stems remain until they are consumed by the fires that regularly rage across the Serengeti heartlands. In the aftermath of a fire the land lies black. Yet all it needs is one brief shower to revive the ravaged plains. The grass grows quickly – shooting up at the rate of an inch or more in 24 hours – and within days the first gazelles are back, nibbling eagerly at the fresh new growth.

Every grazer has its part to play in the hierarchy of the grasses. When the migrating herds move into the long-grass country it is always the zebras that are in the vanguard, chomping down the coarse, tall stems. With cutting teeth in both jaws and a digestive system that can cope with such a high-fibre diet, the zebras pave the way for the more selective feeders.

Next come the wildebeest, which prefer a diet with more leaf and less stem than the zebras. As they munch and trample their way through the sea of red oat they open up the grasslands for topi and Coke's hartebeest with their long, narrow muzzles and mobile lips, Thomson's gazelles, which nibble at the shoots of star grass and guinea grass, and Grant's gazelles, which pluck at shrubs and herbs ignored by the pure grazers.

Nothing is wasted. Even after the migrating herds have moved on armies of termites and dung beetles are silently at work, burying the legacy of scattered droppings and enriching the plains in readiness for the next season of birth and renewal. So it continues, an endless cycle in which rains and grasses, grazers and predators all play their part in maintaining this precarious paradise.

February 23

Gol Kopjes

East of Naabi Hill a well-used track descends a wide slope before climbing a gentle rise and heading out across the short-grass plains to the Gol Kopjes. At the bottom of the slope grows a stunted acacia, its top bent over to form an arch of leaves, and a male lion is resting there beside the carcass of a half-eaten Grant's gazelle.

He is an old lion, his scarred grey hide mapped with thorny shadows. He has a fine dark mane, but his canines are blunt and yellowed and some of his incisors are missing. It seems improbable that he managed to surprise so wary and swift an animal as a Grant's gazelle on the open plains; it is more likely that he has stolen it, chasing away the cheetah that killed it and then dragging the carcass to the shelter of the tree to eat at leisure.

Although he has clearly eaten his fill he seems ill at ease, raising his shaggy head from time to time and staring nervously into the far distance as if half expecting to see his enemies strutting towards him through the grass. His is not the confident behaviour of a pride male. Almost certainly he is an outcast – perhaps from the Naabi Hill pride – or an exile from the Gol Kopjes, whose rounded granite outlines he can see on the northern horizon some 10 kilometres away.

The Gol Kopjes are scattered over 100 square kilometres of the plains. Islands in a sea of grass, they form a rocky archipelago whose clefts and caves and vantage-points have been used by untold generations of lions, leopards and cheetahs. Grey and weather-stained, each lonely outcrop is a closed and secret world of its own, a place of refuge for all kinds of creatures: cobras, red and blue agama lizards, leopards, caracals, hyrax, barn owls and lanner falcons.

To drive out to the Gol Kopjes on a clear February morning when the wildebeest are on the plains is to see the Serengeti at its very best. The numbers of animals are staggering. When you come close they toss their heads and gallop away over the grass, opening up a path in front of you. Then, behind, you see that others have moved in, enclosing you like a living tide.

Even above the whine of a Land Cruiser engine you can hear the demented alarm calls of crowned plovers as they fly overhead on black and white wings. But only when you stop on a high ridge to scan the distant slopes for cats can you truly appreciate the sounds of the short-grass plains.

At first you hear only silence, deep as a well. Then, from the multitudes below, comes the insistent squealing of zebra stallions calling to their mares or challenging rivals, the keening cries of black-backed jackals, the sad, piping notes of larks and pipits, and above and beneath it all, like surf on a distant shore, the mumblings and gruntings of the wildebeest.

The views from the Gol Kopjes are immensely wide. To the south lies Naabi Hill, sprawled on the sunlit plains like a sleeping lion. To the north stand the Barafu Kopjes, whose name means 'ice', where chill winds blow; and to the west are the Simba Kopjes with the Nyaraboro Hills beyond. During the rains all these areas attract lions. The Barafu Kopjes are home to a pride of five lionesses, their cubs and two pride males. To the west live the 28 lions of the Moru Kopjes – perhaps the biggest pride hereabouts. Most of the lions, however, are nomads.

The fortunes of the Gol pride swing constantly between feast and famine, but now is the best time to see them as they return to the kopjes after a night's hunting, walking slowly through the dew with red muzzles and heavy bellies, or to find them slumped among the rocks, gazing out over the plains with far-seeing eyes.

When the dry season returns they will be forced to abandon the kopjes and retreat into the woodlands to the north and west. But now, and for a while yet, this is their land – their kingdom of the grass.

February 28

Gol Kopjes

Between the Gol Kopjes the land rises and falls like an ocean swell, forming wide, gentle valleys where large numbers of Thomson's gazelles gather during the rains to feed on the fresh green turf. The main tide of wildebeest that were here a few days ago have moved on south towards Olduvai, and those still left scattered among the kopjes with family groups of zebras and hartebeest are now greatly outnumbered by the influx of gazelles. Inevitably, the presence of so many gazelles is irresistible to the cheetahs, including solitary individuals and coalitions of males.

One such trio seems to have taken up residence here and have been regularly scent-marking rocks and termite mounds to stake out their territory. Within their new domain is a prominent kopje set on a long crest of grass. Some of its rocks are as big as houses. Wild hibiscus flower at their feet and aloes with fleshy, frosty-blue leaves sprout from numerous crevices. A few flimsy acacias have also taken root, together with one or two gnarled old fig trees.

Dappled shadows fall from the biggest tree, spilling across a dome of rock on which the three cheetahs are taking their ease. Above them sits the hunched figure of a Verreaux's eagle owl, a ghostly grey creature as tall as a man's arm with finely barred chest feathers and startling pink eyelids. From time to time the bird opens its eyes and stares down at the resting cats, but they ignore him. Their own gaze is fixed on the sunlit valley below, where herds of Thomson's gazelles are feeding.

For the time being the gazelles are safe. The three cheetahs killed yesterday and are in no mood to leave the shade while the plains lie drugged with heat. Besides, there is no hurry. Later, when the air grows cooler as the sun begins its swift descent beyond the Itonjo Hills, the gazelles will still be there.

All three cheetahs are in peak condition, with deep chests, glossy coats and long, white-tipped tails. Like most members of such coalitions they are noticeably bigger than solitary males, each weighing at least five kilograms more than the average loner. Almost certainly they are brothers, litter-mates who will probably stay together for the rest of their days. Dr Tim Caro, a biologist who studied Serengeti cheetahs in the 1980s, found that litter-mates tend to look more alike than other cheetahs. In particular, the widths of the black and white bands on their tails are often similar, and this is certainly true of the handsome trio under the fig tree.

The three cheetahs pass the heat of the day in sleep. Beneath the fig tree's protective canopy their spotted coats blend so perfectly with the interplay of light and shadow that it would be easy to drive past and never know they were there. Only when an ear twitches or a white tail-tip rises and falls with a soft thump is their presence revealed. Sometimes, when a fly settles on the white fur of their bellies, a bold agamid lizard darts forward to snap it up and then quickly scuttles away. Otherwise, apart from occasional flurries of wattled starlings, nothing stirs.

In the late afternoon one of the cheetahs lifts his head and instantly becomes alert. A sudden movement has caught his eyes. One moment the gazelles in the valley below were feeding peacefully. The next, all heads were up, and those farthest from the kopje began to race over the grass like flurries of wind-blown leaves.

The gazelles had been spooked by another cheetah walking over a distant ridge. For a moment it stood against the sky, its tail held in an upturned arc as it watched the fleeing gazelles. Now, unaware of the watching brothers, it is walking slowly towards their kopje. All three brothers have risen to their feet but do not move from their shade tree. They wait until the lone cheetah is less than 200 metres away, then step out into the bright sunlight.

Too late the cheetah sees them coming. They walk slowly, shoulder to shoulder, with heads held low and menace in every step. To flee is futile. He can outrun every animal on the plains except his own kind. Nor can he offer much of a fight — the odds are just too high. When the brothers are almost on him, closing the gap in galloping bounds, he flips on his back in a desperate act of submission.

Left: Two male cheetahs capturing and killing a wildebeest calf. The most commonly taken prey by cheetahs in the Serengeti-Mara are Thomson's gazelles and impala, but when the wildebeest give birth to their calves all of the larger predators take their share of these vulnerable youngsters. Cheetahs must try and feed quickly before the vultures gather, which in turn attracts lions and hyenas to the kill. By hunting together male cheetahs have been known to pull down yearling wildebeest.

It is no use. The three brothers attack without mercy. For a while there is such a melee of grappling bodies and slapping paws that it is impossible to tell which cat is which. Tufts of fur fly into the air, and all four cheetahs yowl and hiss as they fight.

Eventually the intruder manages to wriggle out from beneath his attackers and drag himself off as they stand back to draw breath. They continue to give voice to their displeasure, moaning softly through half-open jaws, but do not give chase. Blood drips from the stranger's many wounds and he is limping badly. Yet he is lucky to have escaped with his life — such fights are so commonplace in the Serengeti that no more than half of all males who reach adolescence survive to old age.

At sundown, the encounter forgotten, the brothers bowl over a Thomson's gazelle before it has run 200 metres. As always they feed hurriedly, lying around their kill like the spokes of a wheel. A gazelle is little enough between three, but the plains are thick with game and they will hunt again in the morning.

Feast or famine. For these hunters of the short-grass plains the rains have brought a time of plenty, but in the Mara, 150 kilometres to the north, it is a different story.

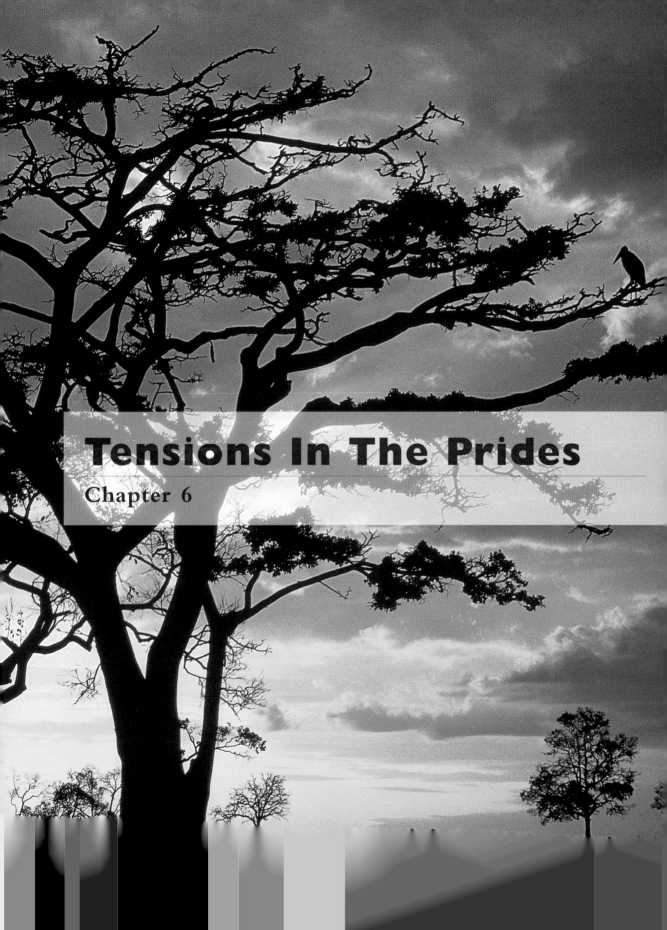

Tensions In The Prides

Chapter 6

March 4

Fig Tree Ridge

Half-Tail's son, Mang'aa, the young leopard who was thought to have been killed by the Kampi ya Fisi lion pride, has been seen again around Leopard Gorge. Leopards, especially adult males, have this extraordinary ability to vanish for long periods. Most of these males are very shy and wander over a much larger range than females. But Mang'aa's welcome reappearance leaves an unsolved mystery. Now he is known to be alive, who was the young male leopard that the Kampi ya Fisi lions killed in January?

Beauty, Half-Tail's daughter, has not been seen for some time. She is now four years old and has yet to produce her first litter. Or, if she has given birth, her cubs may have been stillborn or were killed soon afterwards.

However, the most exciting news concerns Half-Tail herself. In October she was seen mating and it was hoped that she would become pregnant again. Towards the end of the year she became increasingly reclusive, disappearing for weeks on end. She turned up again at the end of January – but with no obvious signs of pregnancy it was assumed that the mating had been unsuccessful. Then, in early February, she reappeared on Fig Tree Ridge with two tiny cubs.

This is where they have been seen today. The cubs are now about eight weeks old and, like all young cats, are very playful. They are insatiably curious about their strange new world and amuse themselves for hours by chewing sticks, turning over pebbles, belly-flopping from fallen branches and ambushing each other among the bushes.

When their mother returns she announces her arrival by puffing sharply through her nostrils – a sound known as 'chuffling' or 'prusten' – and the cubs greet her with an ecstasy of rubbing and purring, pushing their small heads up under her chin and arching their tails much as a tame tabby does when begging for a bowl of milk.

Previous page: Strangler fig tree, close to the spring feeding Musiara Marsh. This ancient fig tree probably began life when a baboon or bird deposited seeds contained in their droppings onto the trunk or branch of the host tree. Having taken seed, the fig would have put down roots and eventually strangled the life from its host. Sometimes one can still see the remains of the host tree entangled within the massive arms of the fig. March heralds the transition from the dry season to the onset of the long rains, which generally reach their peak in April and May. Soon everywhere looks lush and green.

Right: Mang'aa (top) and Taratibu. Male leopards are bigger and stronger than females and this is apparent from an early age. Here, Half-Tail's five-month-old cubs had been sparring, with Mang'aa dominating his sister through the power of his blows. He then mounted Taratibu, asserting his dominance, biting her neck just as adult leopards do when mating – though not quite like this!

Whatever day-to-day adventures may have befallen Half-Tail and her family in their first few weeks will remain a mystery. But no doubt their lives followed a pattern similar to that observed for Chui and her two cubs, Light and Dark, who were born in the same labyrinth of caves on Fig Tree Ridge in 1983. Chui, the first Mara leopard to become accustomed to the close presence of vehicles, was an excellent mother. Thanks to her trusting nature, many visitors to the Mara were allowed a privileged glimpse of the rarely seen world of a mother leopard with very young cubs.

As Light and Dark had done more than a decade earlier, Half-Tail's cubs would have spent most of their first daylight hours lying motionless in the shadows of the sheltering rocks. And, like Chui, Half-Tail would have spent a lot of time with them so that they could suckle from her milk-laden teats. When tired of their begging, she probably retired to the giant fig tree that stood above the lair to rest and keep watch over the plains – just as Chui had.

Left: Lioness carrying an eight-week-old cub. All cats carry their young by gripping them by the back of the neck. Held in this manner the cub remains motionless, making it easy for the mother to transport it to a new hiding place. When a lioness tries to pick up a larger cub of ten to twelve weeks of age, the cub often protests noisily and tries to wriggle free.

Now, at eight weeks, Half-Tail's cubs will already have discovered a taste for meat. From when they were about four weeks old their mother has probably been returning with a warthog piglet or impala fawn for them to chew on before she herself settles down to feed.

However, it will be another month before they are weaned. In that time she may well transfer the cubs to a new hiding place, carrying them by the scruff of the neck just like a domestic cat with young kittens. If they remain too long in one place the chances are that a marauding lion, hyena or even a male leopard might sniff them out and kill them.

Jackals, pythons, olive baboons and martial eagles are all capable of killing leopard cubs, making these early months a time of great peril for Half-Tail's family. And, since male leopards play no part in rearing cubs, Half-Tail must nurture them with no help from their father, the elusive male whose territory overlaps her home range and whose gruff, wood-sawing cough is sometimes heard on his regular nightly patrols.

Above: Half-Tail suckling and grooming Mang'aa and Taratibu. Leopard cubs first eat meat when they are six weeks old (sometimes even younger) and are weaned by the time they are three months old. But they continue to suckle – or try to – until they are five or six months old, probably as much for the social comfort of nursing from their mother as for any milk they might be getting. Mother leopards become increasingly irritable when they are weaning their cubs, growling at them, baring their teeth or simply getting up and refusing to let their cubs suckle.

March 5

Fig Tree Ridge

Baboons continue to be a particular menace for Half-Tail, especially now that she has the added worries of protecting her new family. Leopards are generally heavier than the largest baboon. They are armed with fearsome canines and slashing claws and possess an astonishing litheness and speed of reaction. But baboons have one vital advantage. Living in a troop, they can usually intimidate a solitary cat like Half-Tail and force it to back down or move on.

There are many baboons in her home range, including one group of at least eighty whose favourite roost is two giant fig trees on Fig Tree Ridge little more than 100 metres from her cubs' hiding place. Half-Tail's arrivals in the area are invariably spotted by one of the sentinel males, whose loud wah-hoos bring the whole troop rushing towards her. Otherwise, however, they appear to be leaving her and the cubs in peace.

Below: Ol Kiombo Lioness baring her teeth and hissing at the pride males feeding on a kill. Facial expressions and vocalizations are a very important part of lion communication. The black lips help to highlight the dangerous long canines, which serve as a threat. Hissing is a defensive threat: it is a warning, a reminder to be cautious. In this instance the lioness's young cub was trying to feed on a zebra kill with the two pride males. When Scruffy threatened the cub, its mother hissed and snarled, successfully preventing him from harming her youngster.

Left: Blond Mane (standing) and Scruffy of the Ol Kiombo pride feeding on a zebra kill. Zebra are one of the most commonly taken prey by lions in Serengeti-Mara. Male lions dominate the lionesses at a kill, driving them away until they have eaten their fill. Sometimes the males allow young cubs to feed with them, thereby ensuring them some food. A single lioness is quite capable of pulling down a zebra on her own, even though a zebra can weigh more than 250 kg – twice the weight of a lioness. But there are dangers. Sometimes you see a lioness with a smashed jaw or broken teeth, doomed to a slow death by starvation as a result of a kick from a zebra.

March 19

Ol Kiombo

In Africa the rains can never be predicted. True, the short rains arrived on time towards the end of October and persisted well into January. In Tanzania it is still raining, but in the Mara the dry weather has returned and there is no knowing when the long rains will begin. Sometimes they fail completely.

Already the plains are drying fast and the amount of water flowing down the sandy upper reaches of the Talek River has slowed to a trickle. The wide Mara skies, so clear and rain-washed a few weeks ago, have become hazy with the smoke of grass fires lit by the Maasai along the Isuria escarpment. The heat is becoming sultry and oppressive. Even the lions seem to feel it as they loll in the shade, tails lashing at the ceaseless torments of biting flies.

Left: Impalas have excellent vision and hearing. When alarmed they stand bolt upright and snort loudly, directing their gaze towards the source of danger. This not only alerts others but also signals to the predator that it has been seen, often forcing it to abandon the hunt. Male impalas are particularly vulnerable as they are often on their own in areas of thicker bush, making it easier for a predator to stalk up on them.

Life is harder now for all the prides. Gone are the days of easy kills when the Serengeti wildebeest filled the plains and every pride member could eat its fill. Four months have passed since the migrating herds trekked south to Tanzania, leaving the Mara lions with only resident prey to feed on. Since then the resident prey animals have become more wary. Even so, the three lionesses of the Ol Kiombo pride managed to bring down a young zebra stallion today in the grasslands south of the Talek River.

The Talek rises in the stony hill country between the Mara and the Great Rift Valley. Once inside the reserve it flows westward past Mara Intrepids Safari Camp, where it is joined by the Ntiakitiak, then meanders on between steep banks overhung by majestic figs and other riverine forest trees to meet the Mara River about five kilometres downstream from Mara Serena Lodge.

The Ol Kiombo pride lions are probably the best-known pride along the Talek. Their territory stretches north of the river to Rhino Ridge and eastwards to the Ntiakitiak, but they are most often seen south of the Talek on the edge of the vast Burrungat Plain.

This is where the Ol Kiombo lionesses set their ambush for the stallion as he came in to drink with his two companions. Young zebra males normally leave their family group when they are between one and three years old to form small bachelor groups. Zebras are always watchful, especially when approaching areas of thick cover which might conceal lurking predators. As they drew closer to the river they stopped to stare and sniff the breeze. But the day was hot and they were thirsty, and they did not see the three cats fanning out through the grass ahead of them.

Nose to tail, heads nodding in time with their step, the zebras resumed their journey, then stopped again. This time a movement in the grass must have caught their eye. Perhaps they had spotted the flick of an ear, for at once they began to snort in alarm.

Having lost the element of surprise, the nearest lioness began her charge as the zebras bolted away from the river. She tore after them through the grass, her feet thudding as she launched herself forward in huge, leaping strides; but then, realizing she was too far away to close the distance, she skidded to a halt in a cloud of dust.

Her companions, meanwhile, had remained unseen as they spread out on either side, moving belly to the ground from one low termite mound to the next. Now, as the zebras scattered in panic, the nearest lioness rose suddenly from the grass and sprang at the leading stallion.

In vain the zebra kicked and plunged to dislodge the claws that were now hooked deep into his rump. For a moment it looked as if he might break free, but then the second lioness ran in and clamped her jaws over his throat in the classic bite that lions use to throttle their prey.

By the time the zebra had been dragged into the cover of a small croton thicket the three lionesses had been joined by their seven sub-adult offspring and a single six-month-old cub, who had been watching from the river bank.

The younger lions were very hungry. All were lean, with ribs showing clearly through their pale coats. They moved in quickly, growling and squabbling for the best positions as one of the lionesses pulled the zebra over on its back, revealing its soft underbelly and the thin skin around chest and thorax.

They fed noisily, their grunts and growls arousing the two pride males, who rose from their resting place and moved at a leisurely pace to a vantage point some 50 metres away. Both looked well fed and for a time were content to lie, with heads up, watching the others feed.

The two Ol Kiombo pride males are well known to the drivers and guides from Mara Intrepids Camp. They are cousins, members of a coalition of six young nomads first seen roaming between Rhino Ridge and the Ntiakitiak River a year or more ago. The bigger of the two has a handsome blond mane. His companion, known as Scruffy, also has a pale mane but is easily distinguished because he walks with a limp and has a bald pate – the legacy of a fight in which he was almost scalped while still a youngster.

From time to time the lionesses lifted their red muzzles to look at the two watching males. When they saw Scruffy stand up and rub heads with his mate they began to tear at the carcass fiercely, knowing they had little more time to feed.

Blond Mane was the first to approach, his stride quickening as he drew close. There was no doubting his determination. He came in fast with ears laid back, pupils wide and mouth drawn down in an expression of unmistakable menace. The females and sub-adults were reluctant to leave but moved aside as Blond Mane barged into their midst, grabbed the carcass by the neck and straddled it with his massive frame. Then, suddenly – as if to leave matters in no doubt – he began to roar, ending with a deafening series of quick, deep grunts.

Scruffy, who had also moved closer and now stood on a nearby termite mound, added his own awesome voice, making the single small cub jump with fright at every roar.

Tempers nearly snapped when Scruffy finally moved in. The lionesses tried to block his approach to give the younger lions and the cub time to withdraw to safety. They snarled open-mouthed, lips drawn back to expose black gums that emphasized their ivory-coloured canines. Undeterred, Scruffy lunged greedily at the carcass. Blond Mane met him head on, and for a moment there was a flurry of paws before the grunting and growling subsided, leaving the two males at opposite ends of the kill.

At first the younger lions were nervous. Watching from the sidelines, they listened hungrily to the sound of carnassials shearing through skin and sinew, the crunching of bones as the carcass was steadily demolished. Time after time they edged closer, only to be driven back by angry lunges from the feeding males. Even the cub was hungry enough to creep up to the carcass, where Blond Mane allowed it to tear off a few scraps. Scruffy continued to rumble his displeasure, causing the mother to bare her teeth and hiss, her tail swishing with unconcealed hostility as she watched protectively over her cub.

The behaviour of the Ol Kiombo pride shows both the tensions that arise whenever there is insufficient food for all and the risks of living in a group. When lions quarrel, as they do over kills in times of scarcity, the result can be injury or even death for younger members of the pride.

March 20

Ol Kiombo

Dawn breaks over the Talek River as in a painting by Turner, a broad canvas of sky streaked with brushstrokes of pink and orange against which a pair of lappet-faced vultures stand proudly profiled on the crown of an acacia tree. With the returning light comes a chorus of bird song. White-browed robin-chats, bulbuls and black-headed orioles call from the fringes of the riverine forest. Coqui francolins rasp from the tangled undergrowth at the base of the acacia bushes, and a pair of tropical boubous duet to each other as they skulk in the thickets, their fluting voices so perfectly synchronized that they sound like a single bird.

Out on the plains a pair of long-legged secretary birds tread purposefully through the grass like eagles on stilts, searching for grasshoppers and snakes, which they stamp to death with their powerful feet before swallowing the broken bodies head first. Of yesterday's lion kill nothing remains but the stomach contents, spread like a green cloak over the ground, and odd bits of bone from which hooded vultures are picking the last scraps of sinew. As for the lions themselves, they must have moved off during the night and are nowhere to be seen.

March 25

Bila Shaka Lugga

It is now more than a year since the two Bila Shaka pride males arrived in the area. They were first seen in February 1995 with two younger nomadic males. Together these four nomads were a force to be reckoned with, and they quickly chased away the two old pride males. Fortunately there were no cubs in the pride at the time as they would certainly have been killed.

The arrival of the four newcomers prompted a mass exodus of nine sub-adults from the pride, including two young lionesses. At the same time the pride matriarch, a 13-year-

Above: Lappet-faced vulture. This is the biggest and most powerful of the six species of vultures found in the Serengeti-Mara region. Lappet-faced vultures have strong, hooked bills and powerful feet, allowing them to open up a carcass before the more numerous Rüppell's and white-backed vultures can feed. They sometimes kill small prey such as gazelles, hares and flamingo chicks, and are territorial and nest in trees.

old veteran known as Grey Coat, disappeared and was never seen again.

For the next few months the males roamed widely – fighting with all comers, including the formidable Kampi ya Fisi pride to the north – until the quartet divided, leaving the two older males firmly established with the four remaining Bila Shaka lionesses. In September and again in early October this pair were seen mating vigorously with the females. Now there are ten cubs in the pride.

As so often happens with lions, three of the mothers must have given birth within a few days of each other. Two lionesses produced litters of four cubs and the third gave birth to twins. All ten cubs were born in January, but their mothers have only recently introduced them to the rest of the pride and are still very nervous whenever the two pride males appear.

Newborn lion cubs are helpless creatures – tiny bundles weighing no more than two kilograms whose eyes do not open for several days. At this time of their lives they are highly vulnerable to hyenas, leopards and other predators and are kept out of sight in the lair – usually a thicket or pile of rocks. Here they sleep, suckle and sleep again while their mother leaves them, sometimes for the whole day, to hunt or consort with her pride companions. But they grow fast. They can walk after two weeks and run – albeit on wobbly legs – before they are a month old, by which time their milk teeth have erupted, enabling them to bite as well as scratch.

The Bila Shaka cubs are now old enough for their mothers to lead them to the latest kill, but they will not be weaned for another month and will remain dependent on the adult lionesses until they are well into their second year. In the meantime they continue to suckle greedily, meowing and baring their milk teeth as they fight and tumble for possession of the fullest teats.

There are few sights in the wild as endearing as the spectacle of small lion cubs at play, pouncing on their mothers' tails or cuffing each other with outsize paws as they wrestle in the grass, refining the skills they will need to see them safely through to adulthood. But starvation, predators and nomadic males take a heavy toll, and half of all lion cubs fail to survive their first year.

Even then, should they reach their second year, their troubles will not be over – as the exiled Bila Shaka sub-adults are now discovering. To survive they have been forced to remain constantly on the move to evade the hostile prides on whose territories they have been trespassing. In the past few weeks they appear to have split into two separate groups, turning up in places as far apart as the Musiara airstrip and the upper reaches of the Ngorbop lugga, five kilometres outside the reserve's northern boundary.

Sometimes in their wanderings they have encountered other fugitives – among them the lonely figure of the male cheetah with the mangy ears who was seen hunting on Kichwa Tembo Plain in November. Scab-Ear has grown thinner in the past four months and is clearly finding it hard to survive. Twice he has been chased off his kills by the young lions, although the gazelles he had brought down did little to assuage their ravenous appetites.

The Bila Shaka outcasts are constantly hungry and their bodies have become thin and ribby. To stay alive they must battle with the powerful hyena clans and hunt almost anything – they have even attempted to pull down a full-grown hippo they found wandering across the plain. With their unkempt manes and wild demeanour they are now true outlaws, killing and stealing wherever they can.

It has been a hard time for all, and when the long rains come, driving both predators and prey out of the waterlogged low ground into the stony acacia country north of Musiara, these young lions will find themselves under still greater pressure as the prides adjust their territorial boundaries.

The Long Rains

Chapter 7

April 3

Mara River

The Mara River is born in a shallow swamp among the dwindling forests of the Mau escarpment, the high country that looms over the Great Rift Valley west of Lake Nakuru. Unlike many East African rivers it flows year-round, entering the Masai Mara reserve near Kichwa Tembo Camp and flowing south for 50 kilometres in a series of meandering loops and contortions towards Tanzania. Then, after crossing the Tanzanian border near the South Mara bridge, it swings sharply westward through the Serengeti National Park to empty into Lake Victoria near the small port of Musoma.

In its tortuous course through the reserve the river draws to it a network of tributaries that run like veins across the open grasslands. The Talek and the Ntiakitiak, the Olare Orok and the Olkeju Ronkai are all Maasai names given to these seasonal watercourses which, in earlier years, provided water for the tribesmen's cattle. Officially the Maasai are now prohibited from bringing their herds into the reserve, but in a dry year hardly a day passes without cattle wandering inside the reserve boundaries.

In the dry season the Mara River's precious waters are the reserve's lifeblood, a linear oasis of muddy pools and rocky shallows visited by elephants, buffaloes, zebras, wildebeest and a host of other thirsty animals. But at all times of the year the river is a favourite haunt for countless creatures whose lives revolve around the presence of water.

Pied kingfishers nest in tunnels drilled into the river's steep clay banks. Egyptian geese honk loudly from rock-strewn shallows before flying off, revealing the beautiful green trailing edges of their wings. Monitor lizards with metre-long bodies of speckled gold bask at the water's edge. And often there are glimpses of a much larger and more sinister reptile – the Nile crocodile – sliding off a mud bank to submerge itself in the river until only its nostrils and unblinking eyes remain above the surface.

The river's largest permanent residents are the hippos, which spend most of their day immersed in its wide, slow pools. All day long the riverbanks echo to their noisy guffaws and the explosive snorts of pent-up air as they break the surface to breathe. Rising to breathe and then submerging again is second nature to a hippo. It can do this even in its sleep, and a

Previous page: Late evening, Kichwa Tembo plains during the long rains. The Mara is transformed during the rains; the grass grows long, vehicle tracks become waterlogged, and days are characterized by afternoon thunderstorms and torrential downpours that often pass as quickly as they arrive. At times such as these the reserve authorities sometimes close certain areas to vehicles to try and protect the vegetation.

Right: Flame lily (Gloriosa simplex). During the rainy season, there is a burst of activity among plant and animal life. Flowering plants appear almost overnight, providing a splash of colour to the plains.

Previous page: Rainbow near to Fig Tree Ridge during the long rains. The sunsets and sunrises during the rains can be spectacular.

Left: There are more than 2000 hippos in the Mara River, which rises in the Mau Escarpment to the north of the Masai Mara and bisects the reserve before flowing south into the Serengeti and then west, entering Lake Victoria. Hippos are second only to elephants in weight, with males weighing between 2000 and 3000 kilograms. They spend the day in the water, often lying partially submerged on sand banks, leaving the safety of pools or rivers at dusk to feed on the surrounding grasslands. Considering their size, hippos have relatively modest appetites consuming approximately 45 kilograms of grass each night, only one per cent of their body weight.

mature hippo can stay under for up to five minutes at a time – although between one and two minutes is more usual.

Some of the best hippo-viewing pools are to be found at the South Mara bridge near the Tanzanian border and at the junction of the Talek and Mara Rivers not far from Mara Serena Lodge. Here, hippos sometimes gather in groups of between 50 and 100. In dry weather when the water is low they lie packed like sardines, occasionally erupting when two quarrelsome bulls confront each other, giant mouths agape to reveal an awesome array of tusks.

Dominant herd bulls – cantankerous two-tonne dreadnoughts aged 20 years or more – lay claim to 100-metre stretches of the river as exclusive breeding territories. Here they tolerate the presence of other bulls so long as they remain submissive, but rivals are chased away with terrifying ferocity. At such times, when bulls fight over sex or territory, their tusks are used to good effect – as the livid tracery of scars on their hides demonstrates.

An irate hippo is not to be trifled with and will charge if threatened – particularly if cornered on land. Hippos may look ponderous with their barrel bodies and short stocky legs, but they can run faster than a man, and their tusks – honed sharp by constant grinding against the short upper canines – inflict appalling wounds.

For so large an animal a hippo's skin is surprisingly thin. Although it has mucous glands – which secrete an oily red fluid to protect it from sunburn – it has no sweat glands, and a hippo out of water on a hot day would quickly become overheated. But as soon as darkness falls hippos leave their river in single file, lumbering up the same deeply worn gullies to reach the top of the banks.

Once ashore they disperse to their favourite grazing areas along the numerous well-marked hippo trails that radiate from the river. Except for mothers with calves they feed alone, cropping the grass as closely as an army of lawnmowers. A foraging bull hippo can easily consume 40 kilograms of grass each night and may wander as far as 10 kilometres to satisfy its huge appetite.

Now, in early April, the long rains have come at last. The river is rising and the hippos are free to disperse up and downstream from their crowded dry-season pools. Some bulls take up residence in rain-filled oxbows or leave the river altogether to seek a swampy wallow in the heart of Musiara Marsh.

The rains have brought a spate of births as cows that conceived eight months ago in the dry season begin to produce their calves. From the moment they are born they are adapted to an aquatic life and suckle happily underwater, rising every few seconds to breathe and then submerging again to find their mother's nipple. Like all youngsters in the Mara a baby hippo has many enemies, and its mother must keep lions, hyenas and crocodiles at bay as well as warning other hippos to remain at a respectful distance.

April 25

Musiara Marsh

The long rains have been falling steadily throughout the month. During the build-up to the rains the Bila Shaka lions seemed to sense their coming. In the late afternoons, when great, anvil-headed castles of cloud towered over the Mara, the pride males lay on the termite mounds overlooking Musiara Marsh, their manes rippling in the wind as they watched the oncoming storms. And at dawn, when they roared in the misty half-light, their voices were answered by the rumble of thunder.

The rains do not fall continuously but burst over the plains in sudden, furious downpours, with the heaviest storms concentrated in the northwest of the reserve

Above: Marabou storks searching for frogs on flooded ground at the edge of Musiara Marsh. Marabous are often seen loitering around predator kills, stealing from the vultures and feeding on scraps prised from the carcass. They also feed on fish, frogs and insects. Nile monitor lizards (centre of picture) grow up to two metres and weigh 5–10 kilograms, and belong to the same family as the Komodo dragons, the world's largest lizards. They feed on crocodile eggs and hatchlings (newly emerged young), birds' eggs and nestlings, small mammals, other reptiles and carrion.

between Musiara and the Isuria escarpment. By the time the wet season ends in early June the Mara Triangle should have received about 1200 millimetres of rain – more than anywhere else in the entire Mara–Serengeti ecosystem.

Between storms the plains are lit by apocalyptic shafts of dazzling sunshine. The grass is almost blinding in its emerald intensity, and herds of zebras go scudding over the steaming, rain-soaked pastures as if for the sheer joy of being alive.

The Mara River is in full spate, an angry brown torrent sweeping all before it. Fallen trees that have lain secure in its muddy bed are now carried downstream and stack up in massive piles against the low-slung concrete bridge that crosses the river on the way to Kichwa Tembo. The Talek River, too, is running bank-high. Swollen by the waters of the Ntiakitiak, its main tributary, it swirls through the territory of the Ol Kiombo lions on its way to join the Mara River.

Whole stretches of Musiara Marsh are under water and the heavy, low-lying black cotton soils have become a quagmire, rendering large areas of the reserve impassable even to four-wheel drive vehicles. Few visitors venture into the Musiara area at this time of year, and those that do are frequently stranded as their vehicles slither to a stop and sink up to their axles. Drivers setting out from Governor's Camp stick to the main roads and head north to the drier plains and acacia thickets.

No such constraints hold back the birds of the Mara, which are swept up in a frenzy of breeding and nest-building. Male Denham's bustards strut across the grasslands, beaks in the air, signalling their sexual intentions with puffed-out throat pouches. Crowned plovers lay freckled eggs in shallow scrapes on Miti Mbili Plain. Chattering colonies of black-headed weavers – buttercup-yellow with black faces – suspend their spherical nests from overhanging acacia branches, while male bishops – grass-dwelling relatives of the weavers – appear in their full breeding plumage of black and scarlet or gold.

Marsh harriers sail over the reedbeds of Musiara, and migrating flocks of Abdim's storks spiral down from the clouds like hosts of angels to gorge on eruptions of winged termites. Enticed from their subterranean world by the drumming rains, the termites provide a welcome seasonal feast for a host of other creatures, including frogs, honey badgers and bateleur eagles.

Elsewhere, pyjama lilies raise their pale pink and white striped trumpets among the grass stems, and everywhere – from dawn to dusk and all night long – the air seethes, pulses and vibrates to the sound of insect hordes: mosquitoes, moths and sausage flies; cicadas and mole crickets; swallowtail butterflies with glorious green and black velvet wings; dung beetles, honey bees and hunting wasps; all pursued and snapped up in turn by nightjars, drongos, shrikes and rollers. If the Mara could ever be said to have a springtime it is surely now, in these frantic weeks of rebirth and renewal.

At this time of year the marsh becomes a vast African fen, its flooded reedbeds growing tall once more to create a haven for hippos, buffaloes, reedbuck, marsh mongooses and myriads of water birds. Malachite kingfishers – tiny blue jewels with beaks like red splinters – balance on the swaying reed stems. Wading birds patrol the water margins: blacksmith plovers, painted snipe and gnomish hamerkops with grotesque heads. Yellow-billed storks shuffle through the muddy shallows stirring up catfish, and saddle-bill storks tread deliberately through the pools on long, delicate legs, skewering frogs and fish among the waterweeds.

The frogs lead extraordinary lives. All through the dry season they remain hidden. Some, like the bullfrog, bury themselves in a muddy tomb. There, its body-clock slowed to an almost imperceptible tick, it exists in a state of torpor, living off its fat until the rains return. Others – among them the tree frogs, whose chiming voices sound like ice cubes shaken in a glass – cling to tree trunks or the undersides of leaves, relying on camouflage and immobility to avoid the eyes of predators. Now, woken from their long dry-season sleep, every frog and toad in the Mara is caught up in the throes of courting and spawning, and the nights echo to their roaring, rattling, clinking choirs.

May 5

Leopard Lugga

The rains have begun to ease a little, but many roads and game trails are still impassable and every rut and tyre track gleams with water. As usual at this time of year, the Bila Shaka lions have forsaken their waterlogged hunting grounds around Musiara Marsh and the Bila Shaka lugga. They have shifted to higher ground and have led their cubs north into the drier acacia country.

What has brought them here is the exodus of prey animals – antelopes, gazelles and warthogs – which avoid the places where the grass is tallest and the wetter spots in which foot rot can flourish. The waving, waist-high meadows surrounding the marsh can too easily hide the slinking shadows of lions and hyenas, so the most vulnerable grazers and browsers have moved on, preferring to feed in the thorn-dotted landscapes around Leopard lugga.

Pride territories are never immutable. Their boundaries are fluid, expanding and contracting with the fortunes and numerical strength of each pride and its neighbours. But above all it is the numbers of resident prey that ultimately decide how many lions can survive in a given area. When the rains come, prompting a seasonal movement of their prey, the lions must follow or starve.

In their temporary hunting grounds the Bila Shaka lions have been taking a steady toll of warthogs and impalas and, inevitably, their activities are bringing them into contention with lions from the northern prides. The small Gorge pride, whose three lionesses compete with the leopards of Leopard Gorge for the best caves in which to hide their litters, currently have five half-grown cubs but no permanent males to help guard their territory. They have therefore moved away, but the Kampi ya Fisi pride is a different proposition. This pride has at least six lionesses and is led by two big males and a younger nomadic male who has been trying to win a place for himself in the coalition. So far the two prides – Bila Shaka and Kampi ya Fisi – have managed to avoid each other, but every day brings the chance of conflict, and the nights are loud with roaring as the rival males throw down their challenge.

For the leopards, too, including Half-Tail, the increase in lion activity has made life more hazardous. Some time in March one of Half-Tail's cubs disappeared – possibly a victim of the Bila Shaka pride. Since then Half-Tail and her surviving cub have been seen less often. Sometimes they vanish for days on end. But then the half-eaten carcass of an impala or Thomson's gazelle dangling from the upper branches of a favourite larder-tree announces that they are back.

May 28

Paradise Plain

Now that the Mara is wet and green again the elephants are no longer confined to the riverine forests and wander freely across the reserve. Out in the open they look magnificent, marching purposefully along the wide horizons or gathering at times in herds more than one hundred strong. Even at a distance it is often possible to distinguish between the bulls, with their rounded foreheads, and the cows, whose foreheads are distinctly angular.

Sometimes a breeding herd will go by, led by a wise old matriarch and including several youngsters and babies among its number. The babies were born in the dry season and are easy to pick out because they remain small enough to walk underneath their mothers' bellies until they are about a year old.

And occasionally, as today, far out in the emptiness of Paradise Plain you may meet a solitary old bull with heavy tusks and sunken temples, his ragged ears flapping like ships' sails as he comes swaying towards you through a sea of grass. Nowadays these Mara tuskers are generally docile and approachable, but their very size commands respect and it is prudent to remember that a charging elephant can always outrun the fastest human.

Old ivory trade records indicate that elephants were common in the Mara until quite late in the nineteenth century. Then, in the years that followed, they were almost hunted out of existence, and their absence was soon reflected in the changed appearance of the landscape as grassland reverted to bush and forest. It is hard to believe that even as late as the 1940s thick bush covered much of what are now the red-oat grasslands of the Mara Triangle. Subsequently, regular burning by Maasai herdsmen and honey hunters greatly reduced these savannah woodlands, creating the immense open vistas of today.

As the elephants returned they also began to play a major role in opening up the newly-created reserve, pushing down mature trees, trampling through the acacia bushes and plucking up seedlings. This in turn encouraged rank stands of grasses to spread into the thickets, making them more vulnerable to the fierce dry-season fires that sweep the reserve for days on end.

In 1984, when the ivory trade still flourished, some 400 elephants fled across the Tanzanian border to the Masai Mara to evade the poaching gangs that had almost succeeded in exterminating the Serengeti herds. Swollen by this influx of refugees, the Mara's elephant population rose to about 1000 in the early 1990s and then appeared to stabilize. By now, elephant poachers no longer roamed the Serengeti. The international ivory trade, banned in 1989, was a thing of the past, and in 1993 – when a severe drought gripped the Mara – many elephants returned to their former Serengeti haunts.

Today there are still about 1000 elephants in the Mara. Their favoured feeding areas are around Kichwa Tembo and Musiara in the north and in the Ngama Hills between Keekorok Lodge and the Sekenani gate in the east. In the rainy season they wander more widely, moving out of the reserve towards Aitong and even climbing the Isuria escarpment to feed on the high ground that stretches westward towards Lolgorien.

At this time of year elephants eat vast amounts of grass. Every day an adult bull needs to consume around 300 kilograms of fodder to sustain its five-tonne bulk, but as part of their diet they also keenly seek out acacia seedlings left untrampled by the migrating wildebeest, deftly curling the tips of their trunks around the stems and snapping the roots with a powerful nudge of their massive forefeet. It is not without reason that elephants are sometimes called the architects of the savannah.

Right: Elephants in the Mara Triangle, feeding among long red-oat grass – late in the rainy season. Elephants live in family groups of related females and their offspring, led by the eldest cow known as the matriach. Females stay in their natal herd to breed, while young males leave at puberty and join the bachelor community when they are between 12 and 15 years old. Elephants spend up to 16 hours a day feeding, consuming the equivalent of five per cent of their body weight or 150–300 kilograms of vegetation.

The Great Migration

Chapter 8

June 10

Gol Kopjes, Serengeti

In the Mara the plains are still wet and green, but south of the border in Tanzania a dramatic change is taking place. In the Serengeti the rainy season has almost ended. Sporadic showers still sweep across the northern woodlands, replenishing the Bologonja River and the upper reaches of the Grumeti, but farther south the river levels are sinking fast. Already the seasonal streams have ceased to flow, leaving only a few muddy pools in the Simiyu River.

In the southern Serengeti it has not rained for weeks, and the lush carpet that greeted the arrival of the wildebeest herds in December is now a threadbare expanse of yellow stubble and trampled earth. One by one the last waterholes have dried up, compelling the swift flights of doves and sandgrouse to quench their thirst elsewhere. Even the hyenas have abandoned their daytime wallows and now seek shelter from the heat in their dens.

As always, the zebras are the first to leave. When the moisture has gone from the grass they need to drink daily, and the plains echo to the shrill whee-whip cries of the stallions as the first bachelor herds and family groups begin to file away towards the distant Seronera Valley. Their excitement spreads across the plains, drawing in the rest until a frieze of black and white stripes covers the land as they gather in their hundreds and thousands for the journey north.

The wildebeest, too, sense the change that has come with the dry northeasterly winds and follow the zebra cohorts in plodding columns that stretch unbroken to the horizon. This is the great migration in full flood, one of the most spectacular journeys on earth, which will lead these grazers of the Serengeti north to Kenya, to the lush, dry-season grasslands of the Masai Mara.

Around the Gol Kopjes, where the herds were encamped in such vast numbers during the calving season, there is not a wildebeest in sight. The lions of the Gol pride are still here, as if reluctant to leave the security of their granite islands, but with only a scattering of game

Previous page: Fever trees flanking the Seronera River, Serengeti. The name of this tree originated from early travellers who camped under them and later developed malaria due to the fact that they grow near water, which is an ideal breeding ground for mosquitoes. The Seronera Valley, situated at the edge of the woodlands, is famous for its leopards which are often seen resting in the fever trees. At the beginning of the dry season herds of wildebeest and zebra gather here in their thousands to drink.

Right: Half-Tail resting in a tree along the northern end of the Ngorbop lugga. Leopards seem quite content to lie-up in the most uncomfortable trees, ignoring the sharpest of thorns due to their loose skin. But there are certain trees in their range that are favoured as resting places, particularly fig trees and sausage trees which have leafy canopies and broad comfortable branches to lie along. In areas where there are no hyenas or lions, leopards have no need to carry their kill into trees to keep them safe, and feed on the ground.

to feed on they cannot survive for much longer. Already the cheetahs have moved away, drawn in the wake of the Thomson's gazelles. Soon the lions, too, will be compelled to embark upon the long trek north or west, abandoning cubs too young or too weak to complete the journey as they head for their dry-season hunting grounds in the woodlands.

July 5

Seronera Valley, Serengeti

High in his acacia tree a solitary male leopard lies resting. He sleeps with his chin on his outstretched forelegs, a dark silhouette with tail and hind legs dangling. In the half-sleep of all big cats his ears twitch constantly, catching the sounds that float up on the afternoon breeze.

The Seronera Valley is one of the best places in Africa for observing these beautiful spotted cats. Classic leopard country, the valley is broken in places by granite kopjes and winding luggas whose overgrown banks provide deep cover beneath beautiful stands of yellow-barked acacia and big shady sausage trees with their strange, pendulous fruit. In places there are rolling plains reminiscent of the Mara, where bat-eared foxes have their

Left: Half-Tail yawning. Leopards have large, dagger-like canines adapted for killing prey and defending themselves. Large prey is strangled; smaller animals are bitten through the skull or the back of the neck. Leopards are very agile, and when cornered will charge with lightning speed, biting and clawing, raking an adversary with their back feet..

dens. Seronera may be translated as 'The Place of the Bat-eared Foxes' – its name derived from *Siron*, the Maasai word for these delightful little creatures with their sharp, black faces and fondness for harvester termites. In general, though, the Seronera Valley has much more tree cover than the Mara, with scatterings of flat-topped acacia and ragged Commiphora thickets that look like abandoned orchards.

From his lofty couch the leopard may hear the ceaseless chanting of the ring-necked doves as they plead with the world to 'work-harder, work-harder'; but, whenever he opens his pale yellow eyes and his gaze rifles through the tree's flimsy canopy, he cannot fail to see the zebras and wildebeest now filling the sunlit grasslands in numbers beyond counting.

Perhaps seven times in his life this leopard has witnessed the arrival of the migrating herds at the onset of the dry season. He himself has no need to migrate. Wandering up and down his linear territory, which extends along the swampy watercourses with their sausage trees and dense stands of wild date palms, he will always find enough to eat: reedbuck and dik-dik, impala, warthog, helmeted guinea fowl and, on occasion, a silver-backed jackal or African wild cat. However, the

migration promises easier hunting, bringing the opportunity to ambush five-month-old wildebeest calves and zebra foals – most of which have never seen a leopard and know nothing of their guile. For the time being, though, he is content to sprawl on his branch and take his ease.

Only when the sun slides behind Mukoma Hill does he rise to his feet and stretch luxuriously, digging his claws deep into the bark. He looks around, yawns hugely and begins to groom, licking each handsome rosette on his muscular flanks until his coat is sleek and shining. Then he slides head first down the tree in a single fluid movement, sniffs intently around the base, arches his tail and directs a pungent stream of urine at the trunk before melting away into the swiftly falling dusk.

July 12

Seronera Valley, Serengeti

After the initial exodus from the short-grass plains multitudes of wildebeest and zebras have moved into the Seronera Valley. Not all the herds are gathered here, however. Some headed west when they left the plains, sweeping past the Moru Kopjes. Others hurried north and will already have reached the Mara. But the great mass of animals now present in the valley will remain so long as there is sufficient water – regardless of the famous Seronera lions, whose numerous prides exact a heavy price from the herds as they cross their domain.

On their journey from the short-grass plains the wildebeest travelled in single file, with herd after herd strung out across the open country like necklaces of black beads, leaving a maze of narrow, rutted tracks that will mark their passing for months to come. Once in the valley they disperse to graze in the red-oat meadows between the luggas where the lions lie in wait.

Here, not a day passes without a black vortex of vultures spiralling down to mark yet another kill. The lions look up from their half-eaten carcasses, muzzles wrinkling into snarls of displeasure as the scavengers drop in. At first they chase away the vultures, but the cats feed well and eventually move off to seek the shade, leaving the rest to the birds and hyenas.

In the afternoon, when the red-oat grassheads seem to tremble in the heat, parties of zebras begin to head towards the Seronera River. Today an unsuspecting group made for a stretch of bank where lions of the once-powerful Seronera pride were sprawled belly-up in the shade, passing the warmest hours in sleep.

The lions slumbered on, as oblivious to the approaching zebras as of the flies that clustered around their white loins and throats. Sometimes one of the sub-adult males opened his eyes and stared up into the sausage tree above him, where Fischer's lovebirds screeched among the leaves. But the others did not stir… until a lioness sat up and looked about her.

Out in the hot sun the zebra troop was less than 400 metres from the river. The watching lioness had seen them, and every muscle in her body was now strung taut, her muzzle thrust forward, her gaze locked on the advancing cavalcade. One by one, as if at a hidden command, her companions roused themselves until the whole pride was watching.

Cubs and sub-adults stayed where they were, keen spectators in the shade, as the adult lionesses rose to their feet and spread out through the grass with heads held low. The zebras were more cautious now they were close to the river. At their head was an alpha female, a veteran mare who knew that such places were filled with danger.

But, keen to drink, the zebras advanced into the trap. Another hundred metres and there would be no escape. Then, betraying her inexperience, one of the younger lionesses began her charge. The zebras stampeded in panic, pounding hooves throwing up a cloud of dust as five tawny cats hurtled towards them. But the distance was too great and, having lost the element of surprise, the lions could not close the gap. The oldest lioness stopped and sat down, panting hard after her exertions, while the others regrouped, calling softly to each other with low, moaning grunts. This time the zebras were lucky.

When lions hunt they miss far more often than they kill. But for these lionesses there will be many more opportunities in the days and nights to come – and, so long as the migration remains in the valley, there will certainly be more zebras.

The Seronera River lions are well known to the scientists of the nearby Serengeti Wildlife Research Centre. They are just one of many prides whose lives have been the subject of an unbroken study since the days when Myles Turner, the legendary park warden, watched over the Serengeti during the 1960s. Thirty years later the study goes on, and it is not uncommon to see lions wearing radio collars fitted by the scientists. The sight of a wild lion wearing a collar was more than Turner could stomach – yet even he acknowledged the wealth of data gathered over the years by the scientists and field researchers, information that has contributed greatly to our understanding of these magnificent carnivores.

Without their expertise the disease that decimated the Seronera River pride as it swept through both the Serengeti and Masai Mara lion populations in 1995 might have remained a mystery. The epidemic was eventually identified as a virulent mutation of canine distemper that originated among the domestic dogs of the Maasai and somehow managed to jump the species barrier, killing at least a hundred lions and infecting hundreds more before passing its peak. Meanwhile, for the survivors, life continues as before.

August 3

Nyamuma Hills, Serengeti

The dry season is tightening its grip. Towards the end of July the zebras began to leave the Seronera Valley, following the westward-flowing rivers in the direction of Lake Victoria. Unlike the massed chaos of the wildebeest herds, the smaller numbers of zebras travel in more orderly fashion. Theirs is a sedate advance, spearheading the general thrust of the Serengeti migration across the Musabi Plain into the park's Western Corridor, which follows the Grumeti River almost as far as the shores of Lake Victoria.

No two wildebeest migrations are ever the same. True, certain factors remain constant – the rut in May and the season of birth in January and February – giving shape and purpose to the annual cycle. But above all it is the pattern of rainfall that determines how the great herds will ebb and flow across the park. Some years it is so wet and green in the Serengeti that few wildebeest need to migrate as far north as the Mara. In other years, visitors hoping to see the herds massed at calving time on the short-grass plains are disappointed because untimely drought has driven them back into the woodlands to the west.

The rain and the grass – these are the twin stars that the wildebeest follow from the day they are born. When thunderclouds trail pillars of rain across the horizon they can travel swiftly for hour after hour, drawn by the promise of fresh grazing perhaps 50 kilometres away. When they canter, so finely tuned are their bodies that they use no more energy than when walking. Ungainly they may be, even comical with their absurd, capering gait, but no animal is more perfectly suited to a life on the move than these indomitable long-distance travellers.

Every year a wildebeest of the Serengeti faces an individual odyssey of up to 3000 kilometres, yet the dynamics of these epic journeys are still not fully understood. What strange compulsion urges them to cross Lake Lagarja, on the southern edges of the park, when they could simply walk around it? Yet some years they cross and re-cross in their tens of thousands, leaving thousands of drowned calves in their wake.

Even when the great migration follows what is thought to be its most predictable pattern the herds wander this way and that, splitting and regrouping as they go. Sometimes they disperse for days to feed or even retrace their steps as they chase the rains, but the momentum is never lost for long. Harassed by the slouching hyenas, ambushed by lion prides, they swirl on past the Nyamuma Hills, rivers of animals running flank to flank, seeking their own separate ways through the valleys and defiles of the Western Corridor.

The Western Corridor is a wild and remote stretch of the park, seldom visited by tourists but regularly entered by gangs of meat poachers whose cruel snares, made from

Right: The martial eagle is the largest African eagle. Females are larger than males, and are more heavily spotted on the breast. They prey on game birds, monitor lizards, young antelope, warthog piglets and hares. They nest in the tops of tall trees.

Previous page: Massed herd of wildebeest feeding in long red-oat grass early in the dry season. Wildebeest prefer short green grass, but at the start of the dry season they must plough through the long grass areas in a massed feeding front as they enter the Western Corridor of the Serengeti; others move directly north to the Masai Mara. Soon the long grass is eaten and trampled down. When it rains, areas already grazed become green again and the wildebeest return to crop the grass once more.

Left: Hyenas and black-backed jackals feeding on a wildebeest carcass near the Bila Shaka lugga. The presence of vultures helps to alert scavengers and predators to the location of a carcass. During the dry season in the Mara there is a surfeit of food for scavengers to feed on – victims of predators, starvation and disease. All the larger predators except for cheetahs will scavenge if given the chance; it is often easier to scavenge than to kill. Hyenas can dominate other predators at a carcass except for lions, and when in large numbers sometimes even rob lions. Jackals are very quick and can often steal scraps from a carcass despite the presence of hyenas, though when vultures gather in really large numbers both jackals and hyenas may eventually abandon their meal in the face of such persistence.

lengths of steel cable, trap tens of thousands of animals every year. Here, under the hot, stony hills, are acacia woodlands, vast, hostile tracts of whistling thorn and open plains dotted with spiky thickets of sansevieria, or wild sisal. To the north of the Grumeti River lie the Ruana and Sabora Plains, reaching away beyond the park to the old German fort at Ikoma. To the south, beyond the Nyakoromo Hills, martial eagles sail on hunting forays over the riverine palms of the Mbalageti Valley.

For the cheetahs of the Western Corridor the influx of migrating gazelles from the short-grass plains brings a time of good hunting. Even so, when the wildebeest and zebra move on towards the Mara some cheetahs will travel with them – abandoning the gazelles, which spend the rest of the dry season in the northern woodlands until the rains draw them south once more.

In these dry months, when the blue and yellow hibiscus flowers fade among the long grasses, the Corridor is alive with game. Skittish herds of eland, Africa's biggest antelope, trot like cattle along the ridges, dewlaps swinging as they vanish over the skyline. Buffaloes glower from the riverine forests. Giraffes browse among the acacias and cheetahs lie sleeping in the thorny thickets.

On Ndoha Plain in the south of the Corridor, topi survey the passing herds from every termite mound; and the Ndabaka Plains beyond Kirawira have their own resident population of several thousand wildebeest. The Ndabaka herds mingle freely with their newly-arrived kin from the short-grass plains, but they breed at a slightly different time of year on their own traditional calving grounds.

Seen from the hilltops, the migrating wildebeest look like *siafu* – the marching safari ants which emerge in their millions during the rainy season – as they cross the Corridor's speckled thornscapes in black treacly lines or spread out to form slow-moving clots on the plains. For the oldest wildebeest this may be the fifteenth time that they have undertaken the long trek to Kenya. But among the herds are also hundreds of thousands of young calves for which this migration is the first. In the panic-driven stampedes triggered by charging lions many become separated from their mothers, to be picked off at leisure by predators and scavengers.

Most, however, will survive. Travelling close to their mothers, the spiky-horned youngsters unconsciously absorb the lie of the land – the most favoured feeding sites, the best drinking places, the passes and river crossings – storing the information like a map whose contours will guide them in future years when they repeat the long journey as adults.

August 15

Kirawira, Serengeti

The Grumeti River is the main source of water in the Western Corridor. It begins in the north-eastern corner of the park, in the beautiful granite hill country not far from Lobo Safari Lodge, and ends at Lake Victoria, 160 kilometres away.

For much of its length it becomes a sand river by the end of the dry season, but in the long rains flash floods bring it back to life, awakening the catfish in their muddy tombs as it flows in silvery coils down to the lake. Herons and hamerkops search its boulder-strewn shallows for frogs, clams and freshwater crabs, and its forested banks echo again to the cries of cuckoos, turacos and kingfishers.

Other, much larger and altogether more menacing denizens inhabit the languid pools of Kirawira, a deceptively tranquil stretch of the river that is home to the biggest crocodiles in Africa. Floating like half-submerged logs or basking on the banks with jaws agape, these ancient guardians of the Grumeti are the stuff of nightmares. Some are monsters more than six metres long and may have lived here for nearly a hundred years. The metabolism of these giants is extraordinary – they need to eat only half their body weight each year. Most of the time they are content to sleep, living off their fat. But once a year, when the migration approaches the Grumeti, the drumming of a million hooves sends a signal to the crocodiles: the wildebeest are coming.

By the time they arrive the flow of the Grumeti is beginning to dwindle in the relentless heat; but there is still plenty of water in the pools at Kirawira, and the thirsty wildebeest must drink as they hurry in from the plains. With zebras among them the throng edges closer, faltering, jostling and pushing until those at the front have no alternative but to move forward to the water's edge. Soon, long lines of animals are drinking, their horned heads reflected in the muddy water.

None seem to notice the armour-plated monster nosing soundlessly towards the press of bodies. Almost imperceptibly it drifts nearer, only its eyes and the bony ridges on its broad back breaking the surface. If any of the young wildebeest now drinking have seen it, they pay no attention. For most it is their first glimpse of a crocodile; for one it will be the last.

To the wildebeest and zebras their other enemies are all too familiar: the hyenas that lope after them across the plains; and the cats – the cheetahs by day, the leopards by night, and the lions they have seen pulling down so many of their kind among the whistling thorns. But crocodiles are different, a terror almost beyond comprehension. There is no chase. Just the sudden explosion as a nightmare of yellow gin-trap jaws and bristling teeth erupts from the pool…

The outcome is inevitable; yet the onslaught is so swift and shocking when it comes that it is impossible not to gasp in horror as the awesome reptile lunges forward in a welter of spray to grab a calf and drag it casually back into midstream, there to drown and devour it at leisure. Alerted by the commotion other crocodiles quickly join in, grabbing at the carcass and spinning their bodies as they tear it apart, throwing back their heads to swallow whole limbs with one massive gulp.

For every wildebeest taken by the crocodiles of Kirawira thousands more survive. As the dry season sets in and the pools turn to mud, they move on under a pall of dust, leaving the crocodiles to sink back into torpor once more.

The wildebeest are unstoppable now. Across the Sabora Plain they pour, heads tossing, manes flying, rocking through the long grass at a steady canter, wave after wave of animals sweeping past Fort Ikoma and the Baracharuki Falls to vanish into the northern woodlands on the last leg of their journey to the Masai Mara.

Right: Nile crocodiles have powerful jaws armed with 66 conical teeth that snap shut like a massive gin trap on unsuspecting prey. This in many cases is fish but can include animals as large as buffalo. Anything in fact that ventures down to the river to drink or attempts to cross is vulnerable to attack, including humans. Nile crocodiles can grow up to 6 metres long and weigh in excess of a tonne. They live for at least 70–80 years.

Pastures Of Plenty

Chapter 9

September 4

Mara Triangle

For weeks an air of expectancy has gripped the Mara. After the diamond-bright days of sun and rain the skies have turned ashen as the Maasai torch the long grass around the edges of the reserve. By day, plumes of acrid smoke rise from a score of fires, and at night red necklaces of burning grass glow along the walls of the Isuria escarpment.

A grey pall hangs over the plains, fed by far distant fires as all over central Africa – from the savannahs of Zaïre to the papyrus marshlands of the southern Sudan – the time of the great burning arrives, the annual laying to waste of the lank grass that always heralds the return of the dry season.

Fortunately the Mara has remained largely unscathed, and the fires that sometimes race through the reserve, blackening the plains and killing cheetah cubs too young to escape the flames, have been avoided. Everywhere the red-oat grasses have set their seed. Tall and rank they stand on their coarse stems, as ripe as an old English hay meadow, wave upon wave rippling to the horizon under the wind and the clouds, waiting for the migratory herds to return and mow them down.

In the Mara Triangle the grass is so tall that the cheetahs must lift their heads to see above it as they pad warily on their lonely wanderings. Among them are two large males who have taken to searching for reedbuck in the marshy places towards the river. Other hunters are also busy there. Often, when the tall marshland grasses are still furred with dew, they encounter servals on their early morning rounds. But the servals are uneasy in the presence of larger predators and bound hurriedly away into deep cover.

Servals are the biggest of the small African cats. From a distance they could almost be mistaken for a small cheetah, but a closer look reveals them to be long-limbed, bob-tailed hunters with big, bat ears and exquisite marbled coats. They hunt by flushing birds from ground cover or pouncing on grass rats, mice and frogs.

The two cheetahs are brothers who have stayed together since they became independent of their mother in 1993. The bonds between them are as close as ever and it is a delight to

Previous page: Wildebeest in the Mara crossing the Talek River during the dry season. There is no permanent water on the Serengeti plains and once the dry season sets in at the end of May the herds begin their long march to the west and north, where water and grass are in more plentiful supply. Wildebeest are nomadic, preferring short green grass which has a high leaf content rich in protein. During the dry season they must drink almost daily as there is little moisture in the rank grass.

Right: Dried-up marsh in the Mara Triangle at the end of the dry season, with the Isuria Escarpment in the background. Pools such as this will have provided water for the herds for much of the dry season, but eventually they dry up forcing the animals to travel to the Mara River to drink.

watch them rubbing heads or indulging in bouts of mutual grooming. They have been seen regularly throughout the year and have become the dominant coalition in the Triangle, occupying a large territory which extends almost as far north as the Oloololo gate.

On the other side of the Mara River, hidden in the croton thickets of Malima Tatu, the leopard Half-Tail can see the ever-present topi on their ant hills and, in the distance, giraffes marooned like tall ships in the seas of grass. Half-Tail's cub is now nine months old and follows her wherever she travels. Already it is adept at stalking and has killed its first hares and francolins, but it will be another nine months or so before it becomes fully independent.

The Bila Shaka pride is back on the lugga from which it takes its name. When the long rains ended in June the lions returned from the acacia country to their dry-season haunts near Musiara Marsh. Like all predators they are opportunists, always keeping a watchful eye on the movements of the herbivores. Now, manes streaming in the wind, the pride males gaze south towards Rhino Ridge as if in expectation of some mighty drama that is shortly to unfold.

The great seasonal tide of wildebeest and zebra that left the Serengeti calving grounds nearly four months ago is on the move again. Some reached the reserve as long ago as July, having crossed the Sand River to disperse across the plains between Keekorok and Governor's Camp. But those herds which headed for the Western Corridor take longer to arrive. Now the grazing that sustained them during their sojourn in the Corridor has been exhausted and their restless search for fresh pastures has finally led them to the northernmost part of their range – the Lamai Wedge and the Mara Triangle.

However, one last barrier stands before them – a trial of endurance more formidable than anything they have yet encountered. To find sufficient food to sustain them during the height of the dry season, they must cross the Mara River.

September 20

Mara River

The first wildebeest herds to arrive in the Mara Triangle have remained in this western corner of the reserve, feeding and resting after their long ordeal. Every day new arrivals swell their numbers, having made the passage through the Commiphora orchards and flat-roofed acacia glades of the Serengeti woodlands. Over the plains they come running, the year's calves bouncing at their sides, sweeping down towards the Mara River as if glad to be

Left: Large herd of wildebeest leaving the Kichwa Tembo plains and crossing the Mara River to reach Musiara Marsh to the east. There are favoured crossing sites to which the herds return each year, but when the river is swollen and the far bank is steep many animals may be swept away and drowned or trampled underfoot in their attempt to scale the muddy banks. Each year thousands of wildebeest are killed in this manner, but they represent only a tiny proportion of the total population numbering 1.5 million.

Left: Crocodiles feeding on a zebra, killed while attempting to cross the Mara River. Unable to chew their food, crocodiles must tear and twist chunks of meat from a carcass, swallowing portions whole and allowing their powerful digestive juices to break them down. Having gorged themselves, larger crocodiles can go for weeks, even months, without feeding again, due to their slow metabolism.

free of the thorny woodlands with their lurking shadows and swarming tsetse flies.

Here, on a wide bend of the river, the herds are converging at one of their regular crossing-places. Another big crossing took place several days ago, and already the air is thick with the stench of rotting flesh.

The riversides resemble the aftermath of a battle, with the dead and dying piled in the mud at the foot of the banks. Other corpses have come to rest against half-submerged branches or lie like smooth grey boulders in the shallows, where vultures dance on their bloated bellies. The first to arrive have already gorged themselves and stand crook-winged along the banks, almost too full to fly. Others sit in the trees, expectantly awaiting their turn. And all the while more are gliding in.

With them come other carrion-eaters. Tawny eagles and black kites swoop overhead, crying with querulous, keening voices. Marabou storks – ghoulish birds with leprous skulls and dangling pink throat pouches – stab at the drowned corpses with great, dagger-like bills, and spotted hyenas lope in from the plains. Kites, vultures, storks, hyenas – all have been summoned to the feast by the billowing dust clouds that invariably accompany a big river crossing.

The scene is becoming one of indescribable confusion. On the far bank, zebras that have made the crossing call anxiously to family members that have yet to join them. Beyond, long lines of wildebeest, shiny grey bodies still wet from their ordeal in the river, are rocking away over the plain. Others hang back, as if waiting for the great mass of animals to swim across before resuming their journey.

The noise on the south bank is overwhelming – an insistent honking, grunting chorus that bursts in waves upon the ears. Occasionally there comes a lull in which other sounds can be heard: the buzzing of flies among the crush of bodies or the chatter of Rüppell's long-tailed starlings as they swoop through the dust on violet wings.

Then the wildebeest begin to moan again, a doleful choir thousands strong, giving voice to the rising tension. They are eager to cross the river – and this time their courage does not fail them. The herds surge forward as from a bursting dam, giving the animals at the front no choice but to plunge into the river five metres below. Some take off in flying leaps, forelegs bunched under shaggy beards. Others tumble headlong into the water or drop with sickening force on to rocks, while still others become trapped in muddy shallows and disappear beneath an avalanche of trampling hooves. Nothing can stop the wild stampede now.

The wildebeest swim strongly, churning across the river in a melee of tossing horns and heaving shoulders. Some hook wildly at their companions in their desperation not to be driven under, while others draw back their lips in an anguished grimace as they are carried forward by the sheer press of bodies. So great is the confusion that when one of their number is taken by a big Mara River crocodile the event is hardly noticed.

On reaching the far side the wildebeest stream through the deep gullies worn by hippos on their nightly foragings and canter away into the welcoming grasslands. Others, swept downriver by the swirling current, scrabble in vain at the foot of sheer clay banks as they seek a way out of the water or hobble on broken legs among the stranded bodies of the fallen.

Eventually the crossing loses momentum. The black flood pouring over the bank reduces to a trickle, then stops altogether. On both sides of the river the multitudes drift away, leaving the vultures to their squabblings as silence returns and the dust clouds disperse into the blue. In the days to come the whole tumultuous spectacle will be re-enacted many times over – not only here but at other places up and down the Mara River – as the herds cross and re-cross the reserve in their search for the best grazing.

Right: Rüppell's vulture displaying on a wildebeest carcass in the Mara River. During the wildebeest crossings the Mara River sometimes becomes littered with corpses and the swirls of vultures overhead and crowded into the treetops bear witness to the carnage. But nothing goes to waste; vultures, crocodiles, catfish, monitor lizards, hyenas and lions all play their part by feasting on the dead. It has been estimated that the 40,000 vultures roaming the Serengeti-Mara account for 12 million kilograms of meat a year. Rüppell's vultures can be distinguished from white-backed vultures by their ivory-coloured bills and the white edges to their wing coverts; white-backed vultures have black bills.

September 28

Kichwa Tembo

These are frustrating times for the Kichwa Tembo lions. As sometimes happens, the migrating wildebeest and zebra have passed through their hunting grounds and moved on. Now, were it not for the giraffes' solemn presence and the dark knots of resident buffalo bulls, the golden vistas of Kichwa Tembo Plain would appear almost lifeless.

How different it is on the other side of the Mara River, in the jealously guarded territory of the Bila Shaka pride. The two Kichwa Tembo pride males and their three lionesses have had to endure the tantalizing spectacle of the wildebeest armies feeding in full view around Musiara Marsh. The herds have been there for days – sometimes so close that the air wafting across the river is thick with their bovine smell.

The river forms a natural boundary between the two prides, but – if their rivals are elsewhere – the Kichwa Tembo males quite often sneak across and trespass on Bila Shaka territory. When the need arises lions are good swimmers, and in the dry season when the river is low there is nothing to stop them wading across. But so long as the Bila Shaka pride males stay close to the marsh the Kichwa Tembo lions must make do where they are.

September 29

Governor's Camp

For nearly a quarter of a century Governor's Camp has looked out over Musiara Marsh to the plains beyond. Shaded by great forest trees, it lies on a bend of the Mara River at the edge of the Bila Shaka pride's territory. Most nights the lions can be heard roaring nearby, and some mornings huge pug-marks emblazoned in the dust reveal that visitors have passed right through the sleeping camp.

The game-viewing records kept at the camp make fascinating reading. The record of kills seen around Musiara and Paradise Plain show that, of the big cats, lions are the main beneficiaries of the great migration. During the same period last year they are known to have killed 52 wildebeest and seven zebras as well as, for good measure, six warthogs, one buffalo and a male ostrich.

The records also reveal how heavily dependent cheetahs are on Thomson's gazelles. Of 30 kills made by the Musiara and Paradise cheetahs in September and October last year, 22 were gazelles. Even so, these cheetahs made the most of the migration and succeeded in bringing down at least three young wildebeest.

Of the three big cats the leopard is perhaps the least affected by the migration. At least nine individuals are seen from time to time in the Musiara and Paradise game-viewing areas but, since leopards are largely nocturnal hunters, their kills are seldom witnessed. Yet they too took a couple of wildebeest calves, providing them with a more substantial meal than any of their other recorded kills – six Thomson's gazelles, an impala and two hares.

Although the camp's records show that only one buffalo was taken by lions during the last migration, they are killed regularly during the long rains and are an important food source for the Mara prides. Indeed, one of the benefits of living in prides is that it enables lions to overpower large animals, as the Bila Shaka pride demonstrate from time to time.

There can be few sights in the Mara as awesome as a breeding herd of buffaloes. When disturbed they have an unnerving habit of crashing away into the bush only to wheel round and close ranks in defensive formation. Standing shoulder to shoulder, they form an impenetrable wall of bony heads and gleaming horns to protect their chocolate-brown calves.

The bulls are especially formidable. Heads up, wet muzzles thrust belligerently forward to catch your scent, they fix you with a sullen stare, warning you to come no closer. Their down-curved horns are deadly weapons. Driven home by anything up to 800 kilos of angry buffalo, they can do terrible damage to a lion or a human. No wonder the old-time hunters considered these wild African cattle to be the most dangerous of all big game.

Yet buffaloes are fascinating beasts and it is heartening to see breeding herds up to 100-strong again. Their numbers are recovering after the terrible drought of 1993, which saw the population drop from over 10,000 to little more than 2000. That year it was all too

Above: Bila Shaka pride pulling down a young buffalo. Buffalo are immensely powerful animals with males weighing up to three-quarters of a tonne. They have always been regarded by professional trophy hunters as one of the most formidable opponents, with legendary courage when wounded. Lions often prey on buffalo during the rainy season when the migratory herds are absent from the Mara. But to do so they must rely on help from other pride members – it is almost impossible for a single lion to hold down a buffalo on its own and administer a killing bite. Male buffalo are usually 7–8 years old before they breed. Older bulls live in small bachelor herds or are solitary.

common to come across starving bulls reduced to walking sacks of bones. When they died the scavengers quickly dismantled their shrunken carcasses, leaving only the horned skulls to bleach on the plains. In time even these were broken down thanks to the attentions of a species of moth whose caterpillars cover the horns with tube-like accretions, inside which they pupate.

The lions, too, exacted a heavy toll in 1993. As the drought worsened the herds fragmented, losing their ability to mount an effective defence against the big cats. Each day the remnants of the herds trudged down the luggas in search of water, and each day the slaughter continued. But enough survived to ensure that once the drought was broken the herds would multiply again.

Left: A lioness from the Marsh Pride strangling a wildebeest. The killing is easy for the Mara lions during the migration and sometimes a pride will make multiple kills during their hunting forays. People used to believe that lions killed their prey by breaking the neck, but in fact they generally kill by strangulation, which allows them to avoid the horned heads and flailing feet of their victims; buffalo are killed by suffocation.

After they are about 10 years old the bulls become more sedentary. They leave the breeding herds to live in smaller bachelor groups like those seen regularly near Kichwa Tembo and Governor's Camp. Many become solitary as they grow older, lying up in thick bush or resting for hours in a favourite wallow, where they are sometimes waylaid by the Bila Shaka pride.

An old bull buffalo brought to bay is still a force to be reckoned with and quite capable of dispatching a lion with one sweep of his deadly horns. Yet, no matter how fiercely he hooks and whirls and bellows, he cannot defend himself for ever against a determined pride. The longer he fends off his tormentors the more weary he becomes. His mud-caked flanks heave as he sucks in air through flared nostrils and his head seems bowed down with the weight of years.

Eventually the outcome is decided by sheer weight of numbers. While some lions run in behind the bull and sink their claws into his rump, another delivers the telling bite to the muzzle that will slowly but surely choke the life out of him. It is an undignified end for these old warriors, but no more so than the fate that awaits lions themselves in old age when the hyenas come for them.

September 30

Ol Kiombo

It is a common fallacy that the lions in a pride stay together all the time. The truth is very different. No matter how small the pride, it is rare to find all its members gathered in one place. Often, unless they are mating or feeding, pride males are to be found patrolling their territory at some distance from the lionesses and cubs. Lionesses remain together if there is a need to be part of a larger group, as when hunting buffaloes, but at times they too wander off alone or, more commonly, split up into twos and threes, accompanied by whichever cubs belong to them. If pride females meet during their travels they greet affectionately, rubbing against each other, exchanging scents and reinforcing the familial ties that bind them together against outsiders. But sooner or later they go their own way again, maintaining contact with their pride companions by roaring.

Perhaps living and hunting in smaller groups provides each lioness with a greater share of the kill. However, there are also disadvantages, as two of the Ol Kiombo lionesses discovered this morning. In the red glow of dawn they pulled down a bull wildebeest just north of the Talek River, but they had scarcely begun to feed when the first hyenas came loping towards them through the grass.

Spotted hyenas are the butchers of the plains. They are renowned as scavengers but are also the most abundant large predator in Africa. They live in clans up to 80-strong, fear nothing except male lions and possess the most powerful jaws of any carnivore on earth. Their closest relatives are the cats and mongooses, but in appearance they are half bear and half dog. These hunchbacked killers hunt in mobs, pursuing their quarry until it is exhausted. Then, not able to administer the single telling bite that big cats use to suffocate their prey, hyenas simply tear their victims apart. The Maasai, who have a name for every living thing on the plains, call them 'the lame ones'. With their slouching gait and cringing demeanour, their high shoulders and sloping backs, hyenas are utterly without grace. Yet they are key players in the complex world of the African bush.

As the hyenas drew nearer they slowed to a walk and then stopped to sniff the air. One put its muzzle between its forelegs and began to whoop, as if using the ground as a sounding board. Again and again its eerie voice carried the news across the plains, rallying its clan-mates, and soon more than a dozen were hurrying in from all directions.

Once the pack was present in strength they advanced on the two lionesses with bushy tails defiantly aloft. The cats, laying back their ears and grunting through bared canines, rose to their feet and stood over the carcass, which they were plainly reluctant to leave. One hyena, bolder than the rest, darted in and snatched a hank of viscera from the wildebeest's opened belly. The nearest lioness whirled and slapped at him in a fury while her companion lunged at the oncoming throng, driving them back as they growled and cackled in mounting anticipation.

In the end the intimidation proved too much. Surrounded and heavily outnumbered, and without the pride males to help them, the lionesses had no choice but to slink away, leaving the greater part of the kill to their rivals.

In seconds the wildebeest disappeared under a writhing mass of ginger bodies as the squealing, cackling hyenas fought for the choicest morsels. Hyenas on a kill can eat the equivalent of a third of their body weight and their bear-like forequarters enable them to carry off whole chunks with ease to devour at leisure. One hyena tugged loose an entire foreleg. Another went off with the wildebeest's horned head in its jaws.

While all this was going on the lionesses could do little but lie and watch from a distance, their black-tipped tails thumping the ground in frustration. Then, suddenly, the odds were changed. Trotting through the grass came Scruffy and Blond Mane, the two Ol Kiombo pride males.

They must have been resting nearby when the sound of hyenas feeding alerted them and now they wasted no time showing who was master. Coughing and grunting, they charged forward, scattering the hyenas in all directions. The ferocity of their attack exposed the deep antipathy that exists between the two species. One hyena was sent spinning through the air by a vicious swipe of Blond Mane's paw. Another screamed as Scruffy's canines sank into its rump, but somehow it managed to wriggle free and drag itself away. They were lucky, for many a hyena has met its end in the jaws of a male lion.

Then both lions began to roar – first Scruffy and then Blond Mane – asserting their right to a kill of which little was now left but skin and bones.

Below: Eighteen-month-old female, Bila Shaka pride. Young lions are dependent on the pride for their kills for at least the first two years, and gain experience as hunters by watching other lions and joining in when appropriate. Even so, they are initially somewhat clumsy in their efforts to kill, often revealing themselves to their prey by rushing forward before they are close enough to succeed.

Completing The Circle

Chapter 10

October 3

Musiara Marsh

Framed by the shadows of the whispering reeds, a lion's grim visage stares out into the plain where wildebeest and zebra are feeding. It is one of the Bila Shaka pride males, his huge head ringed by a corona of red-gold mane.

For four months he has lived a life of ease in the core of his territory. Forgotten now are the lean times during the long rains when he and his pride were forced to endure the travails of the acacia country with its thorns and stones and tsetse flies, hiding from Maasai herdsmen, skirmishing with the Kampi ya Fisi lions and fighting with his own pride females over warthog carcasses that scarcely blunted his appetite.

Once he was so ravenous that he tried to dig a warthog from its hole. For half an hour he clawed and burrowed, scooping up clods of dirt and flinging them between his hind legs like a dog after a bone. His shoulder muscles bunched and rippled as he strove to reach the pig, and from time to time he backed out of the hole to shake the dust from his eyes before starting again. But the burrow was too deep, leaving him no option but to accept defeat and slink off to seek the shade.

Now the season of hunger is long passed. Around the marsh is everything a lion might could wish for: shade and cover, sweet water from the perennial spring which bubbles in a never-ending stream from the low ridge to the north and, for a few days yet, more prey than his lionesses could ever hope to kill for him and his brother.

Out in the open, where the air smells of grass and the wind carries the melancholy cries of red-naped larks and yellow-throated longclaws, the grazing wildebeest feel secure. But drink they must, and there is no water here. So, towards evening, in the golden hour when the shadows lengthen and coqui francolin begin to call, they draw together to form long, black columns and head for the marsh. They approach in single file – heads nodding, tails swishing – then spread out at the water's edge, where they drink quickly in the fading light before hurrying back to spend the night in the relative safety of the grasslands.

Previous page: Kichwa Tembo plains in the dry season. Sometimes the wildebeest migration does not reach the northern Mara until late in the dry season, by which time the red-oat grass is rank and low in nutrients. There are even times when the herds do not arrive at all, sustained by good rains further to the south which keeps areas grazed earlier in the dry season green and palatable. Sometimes these long stands of grass go up in flames, the result of fires set by Maasai, poachers or the casual toss of a cigarette butt, destroying thousands of square kilometres of grasslands and damaging the woodlands.

Right: Dark Mane, one of the Serena pride males, recognizable by the split in his left nostril and his magnificent dark brown mane. A really big male lion can weigh as much as 240 kilograms. But even the largest and finest maned lions have relatively short life-spans; eleven or twelve years is old for a lion, and males rarely manage to hold a pride territory for more than a few years.

Sprawled at their ease among the ant hills near the lower edges of the marsh, the four Bila Shaka lionesses are watching one such procession through slitted eyes. However, they do not assume the alert postures of cats intent on hunting as their bellies are still heavy with meat from yesterday's kills, and for now they are content to rest while their cubs romp in the grass. Later tonight, or in the red light of dawn when the air reverberates to the booming duets of ground hornbills, the pride will surely hunt again.

The cubs are fewer now. Some disappeared during the long rains when the pride moved into the acacia country. Those that survived are nine months old and growing up fast; fully weaned, they spend less time playing and no longer rush ahead when the pride is hunting. Instead they have learned to follow at a discreet distance, watching intently as their mothers fan out through the drooping oat-heads. But it will be a while yet before they participate in a full-blooded hunt and another two months before they lose their milk teeth.

October 8

Ngiro Are

To travel from the Oloololo gate to Ngiro Are in the westernmost corner of the reserve is to experience one of the most beautiful drives in the Mara. The route follows the foot of the Isuria escarpment, its green-blue folds and rocky slopes falling steeply around dark patches of forest where buffalo and elephant seek the shade. Ancient fig trees stand out along the top, and it takes little effort to imagine leopards pursuing their secret lives among the granite boulders.

On the other side of the track lie the plains. Bathed in brilliant afternoon light, they reach out to a rim of encircling hills so faintly blue and far away that you might think you were looking at the ends of the earth. In the foreground, wildebeest and zebras are moving through the open stands of Balanites woodland, with here and there a lugga or seepage line – more deeply veined in darker green – running down to the Olpunyata swamp. The trees are widely spaced, their crowns clipped into neat parasol shapes by generations of browsing giraffes, giving the landscape a park-like feeling of order and perspective.

Beyond the woodland the plains unfold in a series of low crests and shallow valleys that roll down into the Serengeti, and most days it is possible to find nomadic lions here, eking out an existence outside the pride. The open nature of this far southwestern part of the reserve means that no large prides have been able to establish themselves, and their

Left: Masai giraffe with young calf. A mother giraffe remains standing while giving birth and a newborn calf weighs 65 kilograms and is nearly 2 metres tall. Lions and hyenas pose the greatest danger to calves, though a mother giraffe will try to defend her young with powerful kicks that are capable of crushing a lion's skull. Lions, often at night, even kill full-grown giraffe, and leopards occasionally kill the calves and store the carcass in a tree, reflecting their phenomenal strength.

Above: The Serena female playing with one of her six-month-old cubs. A mother cheetah will at times play with her cubs, chasing and wrestling with them. But in general physical contact between individuals is brief, though they do at times lie close together and mutually groom one another after feeding on a kill, to lick the blood from one another's faces.

absence is one reason why the Ngiro Are corner of the Mara Triangle provides such an ideal habitat for cheetahs.

A cheetah walking on the open plains is like no other predator. Even when seen from far off through binoculars it possesses an extraordinary ability to dominate the horizon. Moving with a hunger-driven sense of purpose, this remarkable animal carries with it an aura of imminent drama, making the expectation of a hunt hover at the edges of the mind like an unspoken thought.

Part of the magic of travelling in cheetah country lies in the long, early-morning searches, pausing on every rise to sweep the lion-coloured grasslands, checking out every dark shape and shadow until the moment of exultation when a cat reveals itself, a thin, lithe silhouette moving with unhurried grace across a distant hillside.

It is not easy. Following cheetahs requires an understanding of their behaviour, their needs and fears, their likes and dislikes. Moreover, they can be hard to find even when they are not trying to hide – sometimes one can search for days and not see so much as the flick of a tail.

Even when lying in the open they have an uncanny ability to flatten their bodies and melt into the background. That is why every fresh sighting is a reward, and, no matter how many cheetahs you have seen, the thrill of finding another never palls.

Of the Mara's three big cat species, cheetahs suffer most from harassment by tourists. Unlike the lions, most of which ignore vehicles after an initial haughty stare, the cheetahs often seem ill at ease, especially if pressed too close. Many hunting opportunities are aborted when drivers try to follow the chase, alerting the prey and causing the cheetahs to go hungry.

Despite such problems, the Mara's cheetah population appears to be stable. Among them are the brothers – the two cheetahs that have ranged widely across the Triangle for the past three years and are still active east of Ngiro Are. They are a formidable team, and it is a

Below: Cheetahs have weaker jaws than lions or leopards and do not have such long or powerful canines. They are adapted to run like the wind, and so do not possess the muscular body type of their larger relatives. Wherever possible cheetahs avoid conflict with other predators and do not scavenge.

Left: The Serena cheetah's eight-month-old cubs playing on a fallen tree in the Mara Triangle; ideal cheetah habitat with its large numbers of gazelles. Young cheetahs love to scramble in trees, playing hide-and-seek and tag for hours.

revelation to see how skilfully they make use of the scattered termite mounds as cover when hunting. Although gazelles are their preferred prey, they have become adept at singling out the eight-month-old wildebeest calves.

Sometimes, when a volley of snorts indicates that they have been spotted, one of the brothers will take off towards the watching herd in a long, angled run. By now the wildebeest are also running, though not at full stretch. They are frightened but uncertain, disconcerted by the cat's unhurried pace. The galloping cheetah may draw almost level with the herd leaders but then slow down and watch the rest thunder past in a flurry of dust.

Only when a calf has been singled out will he accelerate to full speed. Seeing him come the herd splits, the hindmost peeling away from the path of the oncoming cheetah as those in the front race on. At this point the second cheetah – forgotten in the confusion of the chase – appears through the dust, causing panic in the breakaway group as they see it bearing down on their flank.

In seconds the hunt is over. Breathing heavily from their exertions, one brother holds the calf by the rump while the other grabs it by the throat, wrestling it to the ground. Five minutes later, when its struggles have ceased, they drag it into whatever cover they can find. Here they gnaw into the plump flesh at the top of the calf's hind legs, feeding swiftly in the hope that they can finish their meal before the scavengers arrive.

October 16

Malima Tatu

By now the presence of the migratory herds has made its mark on the landscape. The armies of wildebeest and zebra have been trampling back and forth across the plains, stripping their way through grass and thickets until in places the land is as threadbare as an old lion pelt. The loss of cover offers predators fewer places in which to hide – and if ever there was a time for finding leopards it is now.

Everyone who comes to the Mara wants to see a leopard. On any game drive it is the richest prize, and not only because it is so notoriously elusive. The leopard is the quintessential cat, the most feline, the most enigmatic predator to grace the savannah – as anyone who has ever known Half-Tail will tell you.

Her sudden appearance early this morning is typical of these most unpredictable of cats. How mysterious are their comings and goings! One moment there is nothing but a scattering of boulders tufted with sere grasses and tall spikes of leonotis flowers. The next she is there, her glorious coat of black spots and rosettes glowing in the sun.

To watch Half-Tail stalking impala is to understand how very different are the hunting strategies of the three big cats. For once today there are no dog-faced baboons to harass her with their raucous barks, no black-backed jackals with thin foxy muzzles and quavering cries to give her away.

Soundlessly she merges with the shadows of a dried-up lugga – only to reappear moments later in a stand of lank grass. The grasses are so tall that to see over them she stands up on her hind legs for a moment the way mongooses do, forepaws clasped to her chest. Beyond, in a sunlit glade among scattered thornbushes, a group of female impalas and their young are feeding – perhaps a hundred metres away. Nearby, the territorial ram stands guard over his harem.

For half an hour she waits, motionless, as the impalas move unhurriedly towards her, pausing to nibble at fallen seed pods and whatever green leaves they can find among the fast-drying vegetation.

Impalas are the most beautiful of all antelopes. Their graceful bodies, coloured in two tones of caramel, are set off to perfection by black ears and fetlocks, by the vertical black stripes down tail and thighs and, in the males, by elegantly curving horns. They live in herds and frequent the edges of the plains, where the grasslands merge into denser cover. In this way they can change their diet according to the season, grazing when the grass is green and at its most nutritious and moving into bush country or browsing along the edges of luggas during the dry season.

As a feeding strategy it is highly successful. At the end of the month, when the migratory wildebeest resume their forced march in search of fresh grazing in the south, the impalas will stay behind as year-round residents. However, their fondness for bush country makes them a favourite target for leopards.

The low morning sunlight is now flooding between the thorny acacias. Every sound carries far in the windless silence – the monotonous piping of Von der Decken's hornbills, the fluting duets of Usambiro barbets and the twanging calls of a drongo, a black, fork-tailed bird that swoops out of the thorns to snap up tsetse flies.

All this Half-Tail hears, and so do the browsing impala. Their big ears are constantly twitching and rotating, alert for the faintest sound of danger. Every so often they lift their graceful necks to look around and sniff the air. But this morning there is not a puff of wind to betray the watcher in the grass.

At last Half-Tail decides to make her move. The next time they lower their heads to feed she slithers forward, hugging the ground, using every scrap of cover to conceal her approach. The wildebeest herds may have chewed down most of the grass but there are still enough tussocks, termite mounds and dead tree stumps to meet her needs.

In the stillness the mocking cries of the hornbills sound louder than ever. Oblivious to danger, the impalas graze to within a few metres of the concealed leopard. Half-Tail wriggles her hindquarters, seeking the purchase to launch herself forward like a swiftly hurled spear.

What happens next is almost too fast to take in. The herd scatters, snorting in alarm, but already Half-Tail is streaking from cover as the impalas bound away in all directions, leaping high into the air in their desperation to escape.

All except one. Not quick enough to evade Half-Tail's lightning rush, it lies with her jaws clamped on its throat. In vain the impala struggles to break free. Locked in the leopard's fatal embrace, its legs kick feebly for a few minutes, then fall still.

Like ripples in a pool, the shock of the leopard's attack spreads through the bush, causing every impala within earshot to snort in alarm. Soon the commotion may bring hyenas running, and Half-Tail wastes no time. Although the carcass weighs almost as much as she does, she lifts it with apparent ease and drags it to the nearest tree. Three prodigious bounds bring her to the first angled branches six metres above the ground. There, with the kill wedged securely in a fork, she and her cub will be able to feed undisturbed.

October 25

Mara Triangle

First light, and a mist on the river. Lions roaring, turacos calling in the riverine forest – and two hot-air balloons rise from Little Governor's Camp like giant, gaudily-coloured suns.

From the balloons' hanging baskets, suspended in space above the Triangle, unrivalled views unfold. This is how the Mara must appear to the bateleur eagles and griffon vultures on their soaring voyages over the savannah. Way below a herd of elephants march across an emerald green marsh, leaving clearly visible trails of flattened sedges and watery footprints in their wake. Giraffes float between the Balanites trees, casting long shadows over the golden lawns.

Left: Leopards are immensely strong, with thick muscular necks and powerful legs, ideally adapted to carrying their prey into trees. In this instance the Paradise female (as Half-Tail was known before she lost her tail) is taking the carcass of a male Thomson's gazelle out of the sparse crown of a Balanites tree to protect it from the attentions of eagles and vultures which had spotted it. She then carried it into a dense patch of croton bush and fed on it. Fortunately there were no lions or hyenas in the vicinity to see her do so.

Farther off, the glint of sunlight on windscreens picks out a trail of Land Cruisers as they set out from Kichwa Tembo Camp on an early-morning game drive. Somewhere down there they may find the Kichwa Tembo pride and its new males on a kill or come across Scab-Ear, the lone male cheetah, on his solitary wanderings.

Across the river more vehicles are fanning out from Governor's Camp to locate the Bila Shaka lions and look for the young male black rhino – now firmly established in the acacia country to the east – while other drivers from Mara River Camp will be hoping to surprise Half-Tail and her cubs sunning themselves on Fig Tree Ridge before the tsetse flies become too active.

All over the reserve from Mara Serena to Siana Springs visitors are out looking for the big cats. The Mara stands alone as the best place in Africa to see all three in action and, as the legions of migrating herbivores mow down the long grass, finding them and their prey becomes easier.

To the west of Serena Hill herds of Thomson's gazelles have moved into the Triangle to feed on the short turf left by the northward passage of zebras and wildebeest. Every morning finds them nibbling at the dew-laden lawns, and their presence has not gone unnoticed. Wherever gazelles gather in large numbers the cheetahs are seldom far away.

The mother cheetah seen with five half-grown cubs in January is still here, but her youngsters are no longer with her. Now 17 months old, they should be able to fend for themselves – if they have survived. When last seen they were already as big as their mother and could be recognized as sub-adults only by the light ruffs on the backs of their necks. At that time they were hunting together, rising as one from their grassy couches to spread out in crescent formation like the horns of a buffalo – though at the end of a chase it was invariably the mother who made the kill.

Every view from the balloon's wicker basket is filled with animals. In places the plains are black with wildebeest. Elsewhere, in an emptiness of golden grass, lions raise their bloody masks from a wreck of ribs to look up with baleful eyes, while covens of vultures stand hunched around the scenes of other dramas concluded before first light.

The coming of the migration has brought the year full circle. The massed ranks of wildebeest and zebras have provided its stupendous climax in the greatest wildlife spectacle on earth. Now, however, the grass is almost exhausted. Soon, when storm clouds build up in the later afternoons and lightning flickers over the midnight plains, the short rains will return and the herds will leave, cantering south like a victorious army to reclaim their Serengeti home.

So it continues as it has done for two million years, an ancient story as old as the song of the lion and the running of the zebra. There is no beginning and no end; only the golden sunsets and the crimson dawns, the wind in the grass and the long march of the wildebeest as they follow the rains across the immense African horizons.

In it all the big cats and their prey are innocent players caught up in an endless cycle of life and death. Among the lions of the Mara the same themes, with their triumphs and tragedies, occur over and again – the takeovers by new coalitions of males, the births and untimely deaths of cubs, the dispersal of young males from their natal prides, the inevitable decline and fall of deposed pride males.

Scenes like those enacted daily around Musiara Marsh and Ol Kiombo, with their hunts and kills and confrontations with hyenas, have been repeated down the millennia. A leopard sits on Fig Tree Ridge. A cheetah walks across Paradise Plain. Nothing has changed. The sense of the past – of an older, wilder Africa – is overwhelming.

Today the twenty-first century is closing in on the Maasai's spotted land. As the need for land becomes ever more pressing, Kenya's soaring human population looks with envious eyes at the open spaces of the Mara. Outside the reserve's boundaries huge tracts of plains game country have gone under the plough, leased by the Maasai to wheat farmers whose wire fences push back the wilderness. Inside the reserve the impact of tourism – more lodges, more vehicles, more ugly tyre tracks scarring the plains – threatens to tip the balance, diminishing the very pleasures that visitors hope to find.

However, the picture is by no means entirely gloomy. Since the worldwide ban on ivory trading was imposed in 1989 elephant poaching has ceased to be a serious menace. The Mara's black rhino population continues to prosper and all the big cats are thriving. Kenya can be proud of its conservation record, and its politicians are well aware of the Mara's value to the country's tourist industry.

And what of the Maasai, the owners and guardians of this remnant of old Africa? Above all, their continuing goodwill will be crucial if the Mara is to survive in its present form. While they see a reasonable financial return for allowing visitors to drive across the reserve and adjoining rangelands there is hope that their traditional pastoralist way of life and remarkable tolerance of wild animals will not be lost. The Maasai, then, hold the key. For as long as their needs are met it will be possible to set out at dawn into the glistening grasslands, live in a land of huge skies and boundless horizons and share these last freedoms with the big cats whose undisputed kingdom this still is.

Right: Cheetah mother and two of her litter resting on a rock near Fig Tree Ridge. Cheetahs often use termite mounds as a vantage point or resting place, giving them good visibility to search for prey and keep an eye out for danger. Cheetahs survive better outside the reserve among the Maasai herdsmen as there are fewer lions and hyenas here due to conflict with the pastoralists, who tolerate the cheetahs because they do not interfere with their livestock. Cheetahs do not scavenge, so they ignore meat laced with cattle-dip put out by livestock owners to eradicate predators.

Index